As It Was Written

An Introduction to the Bible

Justin Taylor, S. M.

PAULIST PRESS
New York / Mahwah

Maps by Frank Sabatte, C.S.P.

Library of Congress Cataloging-in-Publication Data

Taylor, Justin, 1943–
   As it was written.

   Bibliography: p.
    1. Bible—Introductions. I. Title.
BS475.2.T365 1986   220.6'1   86-18665
ISBN 0-8091-2843-8 (pbk.)

Published by Paulist Press
997 Macarthur Boulevard
Mahwah, New Jersey 07430

Printed and bound in the United States of America

Contents

iv *As It Was Written*

MAPS

Preface

The purpose of this book is to introduce the Bible to Catholics who want to begin to read the Scriptures and need help in getting started.

The driving force in writing it has been the obvious hunger of Catholics for the Word of God. They want to read, study and pray the Scriptures, by themselves or with others, and they want guidance in understanding the Bible, its history, its background and, above all, its message. Many excellent books are available to those who have already gone some way in the study of the Bible. There are not so many for beginners.

As It Was Written is a "first book" about the Bible which presupposes no previous knowledge. After a chapter which talks about the Bible as a book, or rather a collection of books, which comes down to us from the ancient world (and so, problems of texts, translations, types of literature, historical background), there follow seventeen chapters—eleven for the Old Testament and six for the New—in which every book of the Bible is discussed in the order in which it is placed in the Catholic canon (except for the Psalms, which have a chapter of their own). The history of the composition of the various books is told against the background of the history of Israel and of the Church. The main focus of attention is, however, the meaning of each book for the Catholic Christian reader today. Finally, two chapters discuss the Bible as "God's Book" (inspiration, the truth of the Bible) and "the

TIME CHART

World Events	BC	Biblical Events and Persons	
	2000		
Egypt: Middle Kingdom			
	1900		
		The Patriarchs	Abraham (c. 1850)
			Isaac
	1800		Jacob
Egypt: Foreign Rulers			
	1700		
		Israelites in Egypt	
	1600		
Egypt: New Kingdom			
	1500		
	1400		
		Israelites oppressed	
	1300		
		Exodus (c. 1250)	Moses
	1200	Invasion of Canaan	Joshua
Appearance of		The Judges	
Philistines			Samson
	1100		Samuel (c. 1040)
		Kingship established	Saul (c. 1030)
	1000	Jerusalem captured	David (c. 1010)
		Temple built	Solomon (c. 970)
		Break up of Kingdom (931)	
	900		
Assyrian Empire (c.850)			Elijah (c. 850)
			Elisha
	800		
			Amos (c. 750) Hosea
		Conquest of Samaria (721)	Isaiah (740) Micah
	700		
			Jeremiah (627)
Babylonian Empire	600		Ezekiel
		Conquest of Jerusalem	
Persian Empire (c.550)		(587), Exile	
	500	Return (after 538)	Zerubbabel, Haggai
		Reconstruction	Ezra, Nehemiah
	400		
Alexander the Great			
(336–323)		Judaea under Egypt	
	300	Jews in Alexandria	
		Spread of Greek ideas	
Roman Empire	200	Judaea under Syria	
		Persecution and revolt	The Maccabees
Syria in Roman Empire (64)	100	(167)	
Augustus Emperor		Judaea under Rome (63)	
(30 B.C.–A.D. 14)			Herod the Great
			(37–4)

BIRTH OF CHRIST (?7–6 BC)

World Events	AD	Biblical Events and Persons
Tiberius Emperor (14–37)	10	Birth of St. Paul (between 5 and 10)
	20	
Pontius Pilate Governor (26–36)		Preaching of John the Baptist (27)
		Ministry of Jesus (27–30)
	30	PASSION AND RESURRECTION OF JESUS (30)
		Martyrdom of Stephen (36 or 37)
	40	Conversion of Paul (36 or 37)
Claudius Emperor (41–54)		
King Herod Agrippa I (41–44)		Martyrdom of James brother of John (43 or 44)
King Herod Agrippa II (from 48)		Paul's first mission (between 45 and 49)
	50	The Council of Jerusalem (48–49)
Nero Emperor (54–68)		Paul's second mission (50–52)
	60	Paul's third mission (53–58)
		Paul in Rome (61–63)
Fire at Rome; Persecution (64)		Martyrdom of James "brother of the Lord" (62)
Jewish Revolt breaks out (66)		Martyrdom of St. Peter (64 or 67)
"The Year of the Four Emperors" (68–69)		Martyrdom of St. Paul (67)
Vespasian Emperor (69–79)		
Fall of Jerusalem (70)	70	
	80	
Domitian Emperor (81–96)		
	90	
Trajan Emperor (98–117)	100	Death of St. John at Ephesus (c.100)

Church's Book" (the canon, Scripture and tradition, the magisterium, the Bible in the life of the Church). Each chapter is provided with study guide questions for individual reading and reflection or for group discussion. There are three maps, a time chart, and a list of suggestions for further reading.

This book seeks to be fully Catholic by giving due place to both faith and reason in approaching the Bible: to faith, since the Bible is the Word of God; to reason, since the Word of God has become flesh in human words. It intends to read the Bible within the believing community, in touch with the tradition and with the present life, teaching and worship of the Catholic Church. It also sets out to present to the reader the currently accepted findings of critical biblical scholarship. It does so in the confident belief that the lights by which God intends us to understand his Word include human science and scholarship, as well as the tradition of the Church and the enlightenment of the Holy Spirit.

My thanks are due to Fr. David Blake and Catholic Publications Centre (Auckland, New Zealand) for their gracious and generous permission to use material already published in *Introducing the Bible,* out of which the present book has grown; to Fr. Lawrence Boadt and Paulist Press for accepting this book and guiding it to publication; to Fr. Grahame Connolly, Provincial of the Society of Mary in New Zealand, for permission to publish it; to Marist confreres who read and commented helpfully on parts of the manuscript at various stages of composition: Patrick Byrne, Mervyn Duffy, John Larsen, John Owens, Paul Williamson, and to many others whose appreciation and criticisms of the earlier book encouraged me to write this one; and to Frs. R.-J. Tournay, O.P., and Jerome Murphy-O'Connor, O.P., professors at the Ecole Biblique et Archéologique Française de Jérusalem, who read the completed manuscript and made a number of useful suggestions, as well as saving me from several blunders (but who are in no way responsible for the remaining deficiencies of the book).

I dedicate this book to my mother and to the memory of my father.

1

The Book

The Bible

The word "bible" means "book." It is a very fitting name. For us the Bible is *the* book. It is the book which contains God's word written in human words.

The Bible you use is a printed book in English. However, the Bible was not originally written in English, and copies were being made for many hundreds of years before the invention of printing in the fifteenth century after Christ. For that matter, the Bible is not in fact a single book but a collection of books written by many different authors at different times and in different places.

Language and Translation

It is worth bearing these facts in mind. Take the matter of language. Translating from one language into another is always a tricky business. In the case of the Bible, the languages from which the translation is being made—Hebrew for most of the Old Testament and Greek for the New—are still spoken today, but they have undergone great changes since the Bible was written. Sometimes even the actual meaning of words has been lost.

In any case, no word in one language has an exact equivalent in another. At best, translators can find a word which overlaps more or less with the one in front of them. Each language too has its own genius. It is difficult to convey the style and "feel" of something originally written in another language.

For all these reasons, a translation can never be more than an attempt to get somewhere near the original. And each translation of the same original will make a different attempt. This you can easily check by comparing several translations of the same passage in the Bible.

Here, for example, is a passage from the First Letter of St. Paul to the Corinthians, chapter 13, verses 4–7, in three different modern translations.

First, from the New American Bible: "Love is patient; love is kind. Love is not jealous, it does not put on airs, it is not snobbish. Love is never rude, it is not self-seeking, it is not prone to anger; neither does it brood over injuries. Love does not rejoice in what is wrong but rejoices with the truth. There is no limit to love's forbearance, to its trust, its hope, its power to endure."

Next, from the Good News Bible: "Love is patient and kind; love is not jealous, or conceited, or proud; love is not ill-mannered, or selfish, or irritable; love does not keep a record of wrongs; love is not happy with evil, but is happy with the truth. Love never gives up: its faith, hope, and patience never fail."

Finally, from the Revised Standard Version: "Love is patient and kind; love is not jealous or boastful; it is not arrogant or rude. Love does not insist on its own way; it is not irritable or resentful; it does not rejoice at wrong, but rejoices in the right. Love bears all things, believes all things, hopes all things, endures all things."

What the Author Wrote

Then there is the matter of the text of the Bible.

The original texts of the biblical books—the ones produced by the authors themselves—have long since disappeared. All we have are a number of copies on papyrus (a kind of paper made from the stem of the papyrus reed) or parchment (an animal skin especially prepared to take writing). The printed texts in Hebrew,

Greek and the languages into which the Bible has been translated have to be based on these copies.

The copying process was subject to all the unintentional alterations that cannot be avoided in hand copying—try it and see! Some alterations were even made on purpose, generally by people who were trying to correct what they took to be mistakes made by others.

However, in case you are starting to think that we can have no idea what the authors of the biblical books originally wrote, take heart. It is in fact possible to piece together the original text, rather like a jigsaw puzzle.

In the case of the New Testament, we can be far more certain of its original text than we can for any other book which has come down to us from the ancient world. About 4,700 more or less complete manuscripts of the Greek text—as well as texts of ancient translations and almost countless quotations in the writings of the early Church Fathers—exist and have been studied. The oldest fragment of the Greek text so far found dates from the early years of the second century after Christ. The oldest complete New Testaments date from the fourth century. By way of comparison, our text of Julius Caesar's history of the Gallic war, written about 51 B.C. (one hundred years before the New Testament) depends on a handful of manuscripts, the earliest dating from the ninth or tenth century.

Study of all these "witnesses" to the original text of the New Testament reveals that there are a total of about 150,000 differences among the various copies. However, of these, only a very small number can be regarded as of any significance (most of them are on the level of differences in spelling). None of them bears upon any point of fundamental importance for faith. For over ninety percent of the text, we can be completely certain of the precise wording of the original, and for the rest we need not be concerned about the disagreements, which are minor.

In the case of the Old Testament, the earliest complete copy of the Hebrew text which we possess dates from A.D. 1008. However, this manuscript preserves virtually unchanged a text which was written about A.D. 130. Among the Dead Sea Scrolls discovered in the 1940's and 1950's are copies of various parts of the Old

Testament which date from the first century B.C. and the first century A.D. These show that the Hebrew text of the Old Testament which has come down to us was in circulation before the Christian era, but that other, somewhat different, forms of it existed at the same time. Through the translation made into Greek in the third century B.C. called "the Septuagint," it is possible to take the study of the text of the Old Testament even further back.

When, Where, Who?

In order to understand better the various books of the Bible, we want to know as much as we can about when they were written, by whom, in what circumstances, and what the authors had in mind when they wrote. The more that is known about the historical background to the books, the more easily we will be able to interpret them.

At one time, the Bible itself told us most of what was known at all about the civilizations of the ancient Near East, such as Egypt, Assyria, and Babylon. During the last two hundred years, however, these civilizations have been rediscovered by archaeologists and other scholars. We can now read their official records and their literature, look at their buildings and works of art, and handle things they manufactured.

One result is that ancient Israel is no longer seen practically in isolation, but as part of a wider world about which we are quite well informed. We now understand biblical history much better.

The Bible is no longer the only example of ancient Near Eastern literature which we possess. It is now possible to compare it with the literatures of Egypt and Mesopotamia and Syria. The study of these literatures throws very helpful light on the Bible. For one thing, we are now able to see, in many cases for the first time, just what a biblical writer was intending to say.

What Sort of a Book?

The Bible contains a wide range of different types of writing: epic, law, history, lyric poetry, romance, proverbs, prophecies, letters, popular philosophy, official documents. It is obviously important to know what sort of a book one is dealing with, in order to be able to understand it properly. For instance, it makes a big difference to know whether Sir Walter Scott's *Ivanhoe* is meant to be proper history or an historical novel. There are many stories in the Old Testament which read like history. Many of them are confirmed by our new knowledge of ancient civilizations as they come to light. But some of these biblical accounts simply do not square with what is known from other sources. The puzzle was solved once it was realized that in the ancient East as in the modern West, people wrote stories which, though set against a more or less historical background, were not fact but fiction, in the manner of Tolstoy's *War and Peace*. In the Bible, however, even fiction can convey a divine message.

We have also come to realize that "history" is a very broad term. For instance, there is "popular history," where the story, though faithful to the actual course of events, at least in general, may dwell on the picturesque or the "human interest" aspect. It may embroider the outline with details, such as those who listened to the story liked or expected to hear, or it may exaggerate in order to impress them. At times it may border on the folktale and even incorporate popular legends. There is also "history with a message," where historians tell what happened in order to press home their moral or illustrate their theme. In the interests of doing this effectively, they will lay stress on certain aspects of their story, or perhaps give explanations of events and assign causes which more matter-of-fact historians would not.

The sort of history which is to be found in the Bible, and in particular in the Old Testament, varies in character to reflect the many different story tellers and writers who played a part in its making. It will often be more or less "popular history," and even more often "history with a message." All the same, the general tone of the narratives is sober, straightforward and down to earth, very far removed from fairy story or myth. The main Old Testament history of the chosen people from the entry into the promised land to the fall of Jerusalem in 587 B.C., contained in the Books of Joshua, Judges, Samuel, and Kings, compares well with the writings of the Greek Herodotus (c. 482–425 B.C.) who is known as "the father of history." It deserves to be regarded as the first substantial piece of historical writing, properly so called, at least in the Western tradition.

The historical writing to be found in the Bible—or in Herodotus—falls short of the standards of meticulous scholarship demanded of university trained historians today. But it still deserves to be called history. It reflects the outlook, expectations, bias, if you like, of its writers. But then so, inevitably, does the most "scientific" history written today. In the nature of things, every human work—including a history book or a scientific experiment—reflects the mentality and the personality of its author.

The mention of science brings us to the explanations of natural phenomena which are given in the Bible. They are often different from those given by modern scientists, for example concerning the origins of the universe. However, the Bible was not intended to be a textbook of science. It describes things the way they appear and the way people used to talk (and sometimes still talk) about them. And if it speaks as if the sun goes round the earth—well, even a professor of astronomy probably says that "the sun rose at six o'clock this morning."

Finally, we must be careful not to see the Bible too much in terms of history. History is important in the Bible. The Bible throughout regards history as God's self-revelation to the human race. However, as has already been pointed out, history is only one of many types of writing to be found in the Bible. Divine revelation is also contained in poetry, law, prophetic utterance, the wisdom of the sages—and even in what might be called novels. If we try to force the Bible to be only historical, we will inevitably distort it and miss a great deal of the point.

Past, Present, Future

So new studies have enabled us to tell with greater accuracy what the authors of the various biblical books actually wrote and what they meant to say. The Bible, however, is not just another example of ancient Near Eastern literature which happens to have survived. The Bible is the word of God written in human words.

The word of God was addressed to people—mainly to the Jewish nation—"at many times and in many ways" in the course of history. Eventually the word entered history in person as a man, Jesus Christ. Hence the record of God's speech with human beings is not, as perhaps we might have expected, a systematic exposition, like a theology book. It is more like a documentary of the whole life of a nation. At the heart of the Bible is the story of Israel and of God's dealings with the people he made his own.

However, the Scriptures are not merely a record of past events or a statement of how people once thought or felt. For one thing, every time something written is reread, it is, in a sense, read again for the first time, by a new reader, or at least in a new situation. At every rereading, the text reveals new forms of applicability and even new possibilities of meaning, which need not have occurred, and probably did not occur, to the original writer. This is as true for the Bible as it is for any piece of writing.

In the case of the Bible, however, there is more. The whole of the Old Testament looks forward to Christ and finds its full meaning in him, as the New Testament itself often points out. Furthermore, God's word once uttered does not cease to be valid. Men and women today—as in every generation—can hear the word of God addressed to them with all its freshness and power and learn how he is dealing with them in their own history. But that is not all. What God tells us about himself in the Bible prepares us for seeing him face to face. The ultimate meaning of Scripture will be made clear to us only when we reach our true home in heaven.

The Bible in English

Let us come back to the Bible you use, which is an English translation.

Throughout the Middle Ages in Europe, the Bible was read in the Latin translation called "the Vulgate," most of which was made by St Jerome in the fourth century after Christ. Partial translations were, however, made into the various vernacular languages, including English.

The first translation of the entire Bible into English was made (from Latin) by John Wycliffe about 1380. Unfortunately, Wycliffe's views were not in accordance with Catholic teaching on the Church and the sacraments, and they affected his translation. His Bible thus became the property of his heretical followers (called "Lollards"), and the very idea of having the Bible in English was suspect in the eyes of the English bishops.

So when, about 1520, William Tyndale asked for the support of the bishop of London for his project of translating the New Testament from Greek, he met with a cool reception. Tyndale went to the continent, where by this time the Protestant Reformation was under way. It was in Lutheran circles that Tyndale produced his New Testament in 1525, and his translation and the notes he added to it reflect Lutheran ideas. Tyndale also produced a translation of the first five books of the Old Testament from Hebrew before he was burned at the stake for heresy. To Protestants he is, of course, a martyr. Later Protestant translators built on his work, notably Miles Coverdale, who produced a complete English Bible in 1535.

Catholic refugees from Elizabethan England produced their own Bible translations: the New Testament at Rheims, France, in 1582, and then the Old Testament at Douay, Belgium, in 1609. The Rheims-Douay version (or "Douay Bible") was revised several times, notably by Bishop Challoner in the eighteenth century. For a long time it remained the Bible of English-speaking Catholics.

The Rheims New Testament was used, along with Tyndale, Coverdale and their revisers, by the team which was commissioned by King James I and which in 1611 produced what is known as the Authorized (or "King James") Version. This is still "the Bible" for the majority of English-speaking Protestants. It has been modernized in recent times, most successfully in the form of the Revised Standard Version (1946–1952). There is a Catholic edition of the RSV.

Recent years have seen a large number of new translations of the Bible. Shortly after the Second World War, English-speaking Catholics had two new versions, produced by the Confraternity of Christian Doctrine in the United States and by Ronald Knox in Britain. More recently, there has been the Jerusalem Bible (1966) based on the work of French scholars under the direction of the Ecole Biblique at Jerusalem, and the New American Bible (1970) which has succeeded the Confraternity Version. There have also been many new translations of the Bible made under Protestant auspices, such as the popular Good News Bible. The latest tendency is for ecumenical translations, with Catholics, Protestants and Orthodox working together to produce a Bible which all will use. The New English Bible (1961–1970) has some claim to be one.

Chapter and Verse

An obvious feature of the Bible you use is its division into chapters and verses, with the number of each chapter printed in larger type, generally in the center of the page or column, and the numbers of the verses in that chapter in smaller type, generally down the margin or else running with the text itself. In fact, no part of the Bible was written in chapters and verses, and for most of its history the text was handed on without them.

The division of the Bible into chapters comes first. The one we use today was made about A.D. 1225 by Stephen Langton, who later became archbishop of Canterbury. Our current division of the chapters into verses was made by the publisher Robert Estienne of Paris in 1555. Occasionally a particular division of the text breaks it up badly, and many modern Bibles print the text in paragraphs, and with headings and subheadings to indicate its various parts. These divisions into paragraphs are also a modern invention. The ancient texts were written without them.

The purpose of the chapters and verses is, of course, to be able to refer unmistakably to any section of the Bible and to look up quickly and easily the references made by others. When our Lord quoted the words of God to Moses, "I am the God of Abraham, the God of Isaac, and the God of Jacob," he referred his listeners to "the Book of Moses, in the passage about the bush." A writer today would refer to "Exodus (perhaps abbreviated to Ex) 3:6," that is, to the Book of Exodus, chapter three, verse six. By the way, the reference to Jesus' use of this passage is Mark 12:26. Look it up in your Bible.

For Study or Discussion

1. The Bible is "*the* book." What does this mean?
2. What can a translation do? What can it not do?
3. Is what we read in the Bible the same as what was originally written?
4. Are there different sorts of books in the Bible? What importance does this have for understanding the Bible?
5. Get together a number of different English translations of the Bible. Compare their versions of the same passage (preferably several examples).

2

In the Beginning

The Founding Charter ◊ Genesis ◊ Creation, Fall, Flood ◊ Primary Symbols

The Founding Charter

The first five books of the Bible—Genesis, Exodus, Leviticus, Numbers, Deuteronomy—form a distinct group. The Jews know them as "the torah" or "the law" (the name under which Jesus himself refers to them in the Gospels). Another name for them is "the Pentateuch" (Greek for "the five books"). They are the founding charter of the religion and the nation of Israel. At their heart is the story of how God chose Israel for his own possession. The writers of later books in the Bible constantly quote them and refer back to them.

These books were given the form in which we have them about 400 B.C., but they deal with events which took place many hundreds of years before that date. What we have now is in fact the end product of a long process by which the material that makes up the five books was handed down, by word of mouth and in writing, from one generation to the next until it reached a fixed form.

It seems that what might be called the national epic of Israel, beginning with the ancestors of the race and centering on the deliverance from Egypt, was at first told in various local forms. Eventually, after 1000 B.C., it took shape in two somewhat different narratives which are known to scholars as the "Yahwist"

(J) and the "Elohist" (E), from the name for God—Yahweh or Elohim—which each prefers to use. At the same time, laws were being collected, as well as genealogies and rules regarding religious worship, which were all the special concerns of the priests. The priests also had their own versions, more theological in nature, of some of the events in the national epic, such as the creation of the world and the human race. All this priestly material is known to scholars by the code initial P. (Some scholars make further divisions in J, E and P, or distinguish other strands in the tradition.)

At a certain stage, the Yahwist and Elohist accounts were fused together with certain other elements of the tradition. This unified version of the national epic forms the central narrative of what we have as the Books of Genesis, Exodus and Numbers. Some of the priestly material dealing with theology, law, genealogy and liturgy was also included in these books. A little later, substantial portions of the Books of Leviticus and Deuteronomy were formed out of further collections of liturgical and legal material.

These various processes were continued by the priests and scribes during and after the period when the Jewish people were exiled in Babylon (587–538 B.C.). Some time after 398 B.C., under Ezra the scribe, the torah or Pentateuch was completed. The result is a composite work which is not completely uniform, so that the various parts do not always fit perfectly together. For instance, there are often two somewhat different versions of the same story, such as the call of Moses in Exodus 3:1—4:23 and in Exodus 6:2–13.

Genesis

The first of these books, Genesis, is about the origins and beginnings of things. Its opening words—and hence the opening words of the whole Bible—are "In the beginning."

The first part of the book (chapters 1–11) contains stories of the creation of the universe and of the human race, the sin of the first man and woman, and the great flood which destroyed their sinful offspring. The descendants of Noah repeople the earth, and a set of genealogies assigns origins to all the nations.

Among these genealogies is the family tree of Abraham, the ancestor of the Hebrew people, whose story takes up the second part of the book (chapters 12–25:18). The third part is the story of Abraham's son Isaac and of Isaac's son Jacob, who was also known as Israel (chapters 25:19–37:1). The fourth part (chapters 37:2–50:26) is the story of Jacob's son Joseph, and of how he was sold into slavery in Egypt and rose to be Pharaoh's prime minister.

Creation, Fall, Flood

Creation, fall and flood are the major topics of the first eleven chapters of the Book of Genesis.

The Bible does not give a scientific account of the origin of the universe or of the human race. Instead, it tells the kind of stories which all peoples have told about the origins of things and about the remote past before the beginning of anything that could be called history. Such stories (often called "myths") convey ideas about life and death, human destiny and the like, and were originally told in the context of religion worship and often accompanied by symbolic actions.

The stories in Genesis are drawn, at least in part, from the common stock of mythological stories told in those days all over the Middle East about the beginning of the world and of the human race. In their original form these stories tell of gods and other superhuman beings, of their births, marriages and offspring, their rivalries and battles. In one version of the "creation myth" the chief of the gods fights the monster of the deep (symbol of the sea and of primeval chaos) and kills her, and then, with the other gods, forms the visible universe out of her carcass.

As we find them in the Bible, all stories of this type have, however, been recast in accordance with the faith of Israel in the one God who had revealed himself to his people. It is no longer the gods, but God who "made heaven and earth" by his word (Genesis 1:1ff). Other passages in the Bible also make use of a "creation myth," often in a less refined form than in the opening chapter of Genesis, e.g., Psalm 74:13–14 in which God defeats the sea monster.

As told in Genesis, these stories have also been adapted to the pattern of biblical history. Their place at the beginning of the Bible indicates that they form the beginning of the history of salvation which unfolds in the rest of the Bible. The Book of Genesis tells its stories of the origins of the human race according to the plan which is to be seen in the whole history of God's people and of his dealings with them: divine favor, fall, punishment, promise of deliverance.

People in former times had no alternative account of the origins of the universe or the human race, and so had no reason to question the one in Genesis. As scientific explanations became available, people tended to react to them either by rejecting the Genesis stories as false, or by holding that they were literally factual, no matter what the scientists might say.

Instead, we should see the Genesis stories rather as reworked myths which have been adapted to the history and the religion of Israel. They are not literally factual, but neither are they false. They have, for one thing, the truth of the religious teaching which they convey.

The Church tells us that these stories are put forward in the Bible in order to teach us that God made heaven and earth, that he made human beings in his own image and likeness and in a state of companionship with himself which they lost through their own sin, and that he promised them a future salvation. Genesis 3:15 contains the first promise of the coming of Christ, when God told the serpent who had deceived our first parents: "I will make you enemies of each other: you and the woman, your offspring and her offspring. It will crush your head and you will strike its heel." In a similar way, the story of the flood shows us the working out of human sinfulness and the action of God's justice and mercy.

Primary Symbols

The opening chapters of Genesis also have the kind of truth that belongs to symbols. Myths are symbolic stories. They may be factual as well—the story of the deluge could be based on some catastrophe that really happened, but it also has a highly symbolic effect.

In Genesis, the symbolism of creation, fall and flood still works powerfully upon us. The two stories of creation in the first two chapters are not primitive science which has now been superseded. The story of the fall in chapter 3 does not have to be accepted or rejected as a straightforward account of something that happened one afternoon in a garden. Whatever natural disaster may lie behind the story of the deluge, we do not have to see it as claiming to be an eyewitness account of a flood which literally wiped out every living creature except those that could fit into Noah's ark.

Rather, these stories reveal to us the deepest truth about the world and about ourselves. The world, including the human person, is the work of God, but we are flawed and fallen. In the end, perhaps, the most effective way of talking about such things is by means of symbols.

The opening chapters of the Bible set in motion vast themes, of making, unmaking and remaking, which recur again and again throughout the entire Bible. There, too, we see for the first time symbols, such as earth, clay, the potter; water, the river of life; the tree of life; man and woman, bridegroom and bride, which will run through the rest of the Bible to the very end, gathering complexity and density, and connect up the most distant and apparently diverse parts.

The biblical writers in fact went back time and time again to "the beginning" in order to draw afresh from its images and symbols. The frequent revisions and rewritings of various parts of the Bible strengthened these unifying links and tended more and more to make this collection of books, written at different times by different people, into a single book. It is not too much to say that the whole Bible, New Testament as well as Old, can be read as the development of a set of themes which are first stated in the early chapters of the Book of Genesis. The Fathers of the Church expressed a genuine insight when they called Genesis 3:15 "the proto-Gospel."

For Study or Discussion

1. What is God telling us in the first eleven chapters of Genesis?

2. What is a symbol? Pick out some of the symbols in Genesis 1–11.

3. What is a myth? Are myths true or false?

4. In order to see how certain themes and symbols run through the Bible, look at Genesis 1–3 and 6:5–9:17; Exodus 15:1–21; Isaiah 64 and 65:15–25; Jeremiah 4:23–28; Ezekiel 36:33–37:14; The Song of Songs 2:8–3:5; John 1:1–18; 2:1–12; 5:1–30; 18:1–11; 19:17–20:31; Romans 8:18–25; I Corinthians 15:20–28; Ephesians 5:25–33; 2 Peter 3:3–10; Revelation 21:1–22:5.

3

Our Ancestors in Faith

Stories of the Ancestors ◇ **The Call of Abraham** ◇ **The Promise** ◇
The Test of Faith ◇ **Isaac and Jacob** ◇ **Joseph and His Brothers** ◇
The Promise Fulfilled

Stories of the Ancestors

The stories about Abraham and about his son Isaac and
grandson Jacob which make up the central part of the Book of
Genesis were probably first told around the campfires of one of the
many clans of herdsmen who wandered with their animals between Egypt and what is now Syria and Iraq nearly four thousand
years ago. They were family tales and reminiscences, stories
(some of them a trifle tall) of their ancestors.

These stories continued to be passed on long after the descendants of Abraham, Isaac and Jacob were settled in the land
through which their ancestors had wandered. In many respects,
these stories give a true picture of the semi-nomadic way of life
and of the "international situation" in the Near East about 1800
B.C. (the date usually assigned to Abraham). We can, therefore,
regard them as stories of real people and real events. For all that,
however, they retain a strong flavor of "popular history" and even
of folktale.

The earliest tellers of these tales in all likelihood intended
mainly to entertain and impress their hearers with stories of the
importance and cleverness of their ancestors. By the time the
Book of Genesis was composed, however, the chief attention was

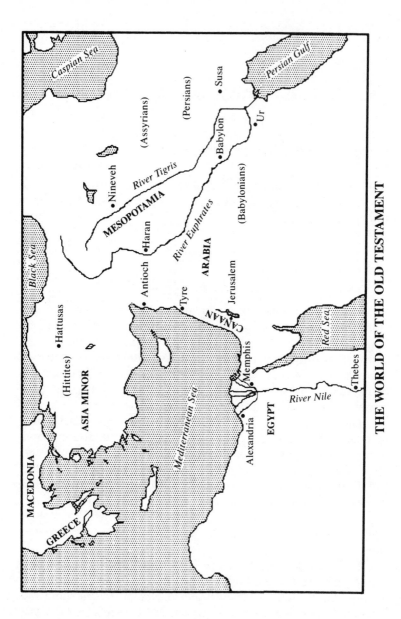

THE WORLD OF THE OLD TESTAMENT

given to the dealings of Abraham, Isaac and Jacob with the God who approached each one of them in turn and took him under his special protection.

The Call of Abraham

At the beginning of chapter 12, God calls Abraham (or Abram, as his name was then). He was to leave his home and country—Haran in northern Mesopotamia—and set out for a land that God would show him. His descendants would become a great nation.

It is important to realize that the God who spoke to Abraham was not one of the gods whom he and his family worshiped in Mesopotamia at Haran or Ur. He is a "new" God who goes out of his way to establish a relationship with Abraham. This, we shall find, is characteristic of God's dealings with people. He takes the first step.

Abraham responds to God's call with belief that God can fulfill his promise, with trust that he will do so, and with obedience and submission to his will. These three attitudes—belief, trust and obedience—together make up what the Bible calls "faith."

It is this quality, displayed over and over again and proved beyond doubt, which has prompted believers down through the ages—Jews, Christians and Muslims—to hold up Abraham as a model of faith. We can see this in the New Testament, in chapter 4 of St. Paul's Letter to the Romans and in chapter 11 of the Letter to the Hebrews. In fact, it is sharing Abraham's faith, even more than his blood, which makes people his descendants. The Roman Canon of the Mass (Eucharistic Prayer I) refers to Abraham as "our father in faith." We are indeed at the foundations of our religion.

The Promise

God made a promise to Abraham. He repeated the promise many times, both to Abraham himself and to Isaac and Jacob.

God confirmed his promise by a "covenant." This was a solemn undertaking made by two parties or, as in this case, by one alone. It was sworn with oaths and celebrated with rituals which usually involved the shedding of blood. Often it was commemorated by a monument or recorded in a written document. There is a dramatic description of God making his covenant with Abraham in Genesis, chapter 15.

God's promise to Abraham was never revoked. It remained the most basic thing in the religion which God revealed. (See St. Paul's Letter to the Galatians, chapter 3.)

The promise was an act of sheer generosity on God's part. Abraham had done nothing really to deserve it. Furthermore, it was not given in consideration of anything Abraham was to do in the future, although he was meant to act in a fashion worthy of one with whom God had set up this special relationship. Circumcision of all male descendants was to be a perpetual sign and reminder of the covenant (Gen 17).

The promise was given by God in return for nothing—except Abraham's faith. We are told that "Abram put his faith in Yahweh who counted this as making him justified" (Gen 15:6). Once again, this is a feature which remains fundamental to our relationship with God. We cannot earn his love. We do not need to. He gives it freely to those who are willing to accept it.

What God promised Abraham was a new land which he had not seen. He also promised numerous descendants who would become a great nation and eventually possess the promised land.

Here was a difficulty which seemed to be insuperable. Abraham's wife Sarah was barren and both of them were old. How could they have a child? Abraham's faith had to be the kind which persists in spite of everything that seems unlikely or even impossible.

The Test of Faith

Eventually, against all hope, the child of the promise, Isaac, was born. But once again, Abraham's faith was put to a critical test. God asked him to offer up Isaac in sacrifice (Gen 22).

Without a word of protest, Abraham prepared to offer up the life of the son in whom lay all hope of the promise being fulfilled. However, God stopped the sacrifice and gave Isaac back to his father. He was satisfied with Abraham's faith and obedience. A ram was sacrificed in place of Isaac.

The story of the "binding of Isaac" is one of the great passages of the Bible. The narrative is austere and heartbreaking. The story-teller and the listener or reader are mesmerized as they watch each action of Abraham preparing for the sacrifice. The tension becomes unbearable. At the last instant Isaac is saved.

The story can be read at different levels and with more than one focus of interest. Abraham and his faith form the center of attention in the New Testament (Heb 11:17–19). One strand of Jewish tradition concentrated rather on Isaac. He was regarded as a willing victim and so, even though he did not die, the "binding" was a true sacrifice, indeed the perfect sacrifice in the sight of God. All other sacrifices, beginning with the ram substituted for Isaac, commemorate his sacrifice and derive their value from it.

Isaac and Jacob

Chapter 23 of Genesis tells of the death of Sarah and of Abraham's purchase of the cave of Machpelah near Hebron for her tomb. This acquisition was, incidentally, the first fulfillment of God's promise that Abraham and his descendants should have land of their own. Chapter 24 is the moving account of the marriage of Isaac with Rebekah, and 25:7–11 recounts the death and burial of Abraham.

Attention then shifts to Isaac's son Jacob, and first to the way he took advantage of his twin brother Esau in order to gain the rights of the firstborn (25:19–34). In chapter 27, at the prompting of his mother Rebekah, he tricks his father into giving him the blessing due to the elder son. In chapters 29 and 30, Jacob is winning Rachel as his wife and is tricked by her father into taking her sister Leah as well, but then gets the better of his father-in-law.

The early storytellers clearly reveled in the shrewdness and cunning of Jacob. And yet Genesis also presents us with a Jacob who is not only the heir and transmitter of God's promise to Abraham and Isaac, but also one who himself encounters God. In 28:10–22, we read of Jacob's dream in which he sees a ladder reaching from earth to heaven and God himself repeating the promise of land and descendants. In 32:22–32, Jacob wrestles with God who will not reveal his name, but gives Jacob his blessing.

Joseph and his Brothers

Jacob, who was also called Israel ("the man who has seen God"), became the father of twelve sons: Reuben, Simeon, Levi, Judah, Issachar, Zebulun, Dan, Naphtali, Gad, Asher, Joseph and Benjamin. These are the twelve patriarchs, from whom the twelve tribes of Israel take their descent. The last part of the Book of Genesis concerns them, and especially Joseph, and tells how Israel and his sons went down to live in Egypt.

Chapter 37 begins the story of Joseph and his brothers. Out of envy they sell him to merchants who take him to Egypt. Chapters 39–47 continue the story with Joseph's adventures in Egypt and eventual promotion to be the chief minister of Pharaoh. Famine drives Joseph's brothers to come to Egypt in search of food. Joseph recognizes them (but they, of course, do not recognize him) and, after a certain "comedy of errors" which gently evens the score with his brothers, Joseph reveals himself to them and invites them to settle in Egypt with their father. Jacob thus lives to see again the son whom he had thought long dead. It is the same sort of story that Shakespeare uses in his last plays, *A Winter's Tale* and *The Tempest,* involving the themes of loss and restoration, injury and forgiveness, estrangement, recognition and reconciliation. Such themes have a fitting place in the opening book of the Bible.

The final chapters of Genesis, 48–50, contain the last blessings of Jacob on his sons and on Joseph's sons Ephraim and Manasseh, and his death and funeral. The book is thus brought to a conclusion with the children of Israel in Egypt, where, however, they are not destined to stay.

The Promise Fulfilled

A certain tension is built into the Book of Genesis. On the one hand, it seems to be a family story and to concern only its members and their descendants. On the other hand, right from the beginning, God's promise to Abraham envisaged a benefit to the whole human race: "All the tribes of the earth shall bless themselves by you" (Gen 12:3).

Furthermore, each instance in which the promise is fulfilled turns out to look ahead to some further fulfillment. The promise does not end with Isaac or even with the seventy descendants of Jacob who went down into Egypt. The cave of Machpelah is only a first installment of what is to come. For that matter, could any actual fulfillment exhaust a promise to make the descendants of Abraham as many as the specks of dust on the ground or the stars in the sky (Gen 13:16; 15:5)?

The Book of Genesis, and with it the whole Bible, is thereby given a certain dynamism that drives always further on, beyond. The eyes of its readers are turned toward the future. The promise of God to Abraham can be fulfilled only in terms of the whole of humankind and of a homeland for all peoples.

Christians reading about Isaac will think of Jesus. He was descended from Abraham (see Mt 1) and born of a virgin who therefore had no hope of having a child (see Lk 1). He offered himself as a sacrifice in obedience to his Father, and in the New Testament is called by John the Baptist "the lamb of God" (Jn 1:29), i.e., the lamb that God provided for the sacrifice (see Gen 22:8). By God himself he is called "my Son, the Beloved" (Mk 1:11), as Isaac was to Abraham (Gen 22:2). As St. Paul points out, "God did not spare his own Son, but gave him up to benefit us all" (Rom 8:32.)

Now we look for a "better homeland," namely a "heavenly homeland" (Heb 11:16). We journey on toward it in the faith of Abraham and Sarah, Isaac, Jacob and Joseph.

For Study or Discussion

1. Why is Abraham called "our father in faith"?
2. What can we learn from the story of Abraham about God and the way he deals with people?
3. Is there a lesson for us in the stories of Abraham, Isaac and Jacob?

4

The Chosen People

The Deliverance from Egypt ◇ **Exodus** ◇ **The Covenant** ◇ **The Law** ◇ **The Holy God: Leviticus** ◇ **In the Wilderness: Numbers** ◇ **The Divine Lover: Deuteronomy** ◇ **The People of God**

The Deliverance From Egypt

From about 1700 to about 1500 B.C. the land of Egypt was under the rule of a foreign dynasty (the Hyksos). During that period a number of "outsiders" came into the country to seek their fortune. Among them were the descendants of Abraham, Isaac and Jacob. The story of Joseph in the Book of Genesis tells how they rose to wealth and power. When the foreign rulers were driven out, the other newcomers who remained were reduced to slavery.

The Book of Exodus opens depicting the oppression of the Israelites, who were put to hard labor on public works schemes and even threatened with genocide.

At last deliverance came. Moses, an Israelite who had been brought up at the court of the Egyptian king, appeared as the spokesman of the God of Abraham, Isaac and Jacob.

Moses and his brother Aaron persuaded their fellow Israelites to follow them and compelled Pharoah to let the people go. A mixed band of Israelites and others followed Moses and Aaron out of Egypt. They finally escaped across the Sea of Reeds (not the Red Sea proper—in fact, probably at the Bitter Lakes through which the Suez Canal passes today). There the Egyptian forces sent to recapture them met with disaster. They then turned down into the Sinai peninsula.

This incident which occurred about 1250 B.C. was of no great importance to the Egyptians. It was, on the other hand, of supreme importance to the Israelites. They looked (and still look) back on it as the foundation of their nationhood and their faith (see Pss 114, 105 and 106; Wis 19; Acts 7). Later events in their history, such as the return from exile, were experienced and described in terms of "another exodus" (see Is 41:17–20; 43:16–21).

For it was God who had delivered Israel from Egypt. He had chosen Israel for himself. Ever afterward, God meant for Israel the God of the exodus.

Exodus

The theme of the Book of Exodus is this: God rescued Israel from destruction and so acquired rights over her, rights which Israel should gratefully acknowledge.

Israel had not chosen God. He had chosen her. Furthermore, God had chosen her not because she was a great nation—she was the least of all peoples—but because he loved her (see Dt 7:7–8). He had made her his own. From then on she belonged to him. He was the master of her destiny. The whole history of Israel was shaped by God and was in essence the story of his dealings with her.

The first part of the Book of Exodus, down to verse 21 of chapter 15, describes the deliverance from Egypt. This narrative may well combine the stories of several different groups that left Egypt around the same period and went to Canaan by different routes, encountering different experiences on the way. Later in the promised land, having become one people, they shared one history (just as various groups of immigrants to the United States have come to share a common history) which was told as literally the history of them all.

After the introductory chapter setting out the sufferings of the Israelites, the story turns to Moses. We read of his birth and early life, and of his commission from God, who reveals his name as Yahweh. Moses is to bring God's people out of Egypt and lead them to the land God had promised their ancestors.

Then come the ten plagues sent on the land to make Pharaoh release the people, the institution of the feast of Passover, the crossing of the Sea of Reeds and the destruction of the Egyptian army. After their successful escape, the Israelite women sing a chant of triumph for the God who had saved them. It is the oldest song in the Bible and could be regarded as the origin of the Book of Psalms:

> Sing of Yahweh: he has covered himself in glory,
> Horse and rider he has thrown into the sea.

The next part of the Book of Exodus, down to the end of chapter 18, recounts the journey of the people through the Sinai penin-sula. At every step of the way the Israelites grumble and complain against Moses and against the Lord—they have no food, they have no water. Time and time again God provides them with what they need—manna from heaven, water from the rock. Still they do not learn to trust him. They are attacked by enemies, but God gives victory in answer to the prayers of Moses.

The Covenant

At last the people led by Moses arrived at Mount Sinai, where God showed himself in thunder and lightning. Chapters 19–24 of the Book of Exodus deal with the covenant which God made with them there. God now solemnly declared that by rescuing the peo-ple, he had acquired them as his own possession. The people on their side solemnly acknowledged that they belonged to him.

The covenant was the final act by which Israel became a na-tion. Those who before had not been a people were now a people, the people of God. From first to last it was God's doing. Further-more, God's promise and his choice were made forever. On the other hand, this covenant would last only so long as Israel ob-served its conditions.

Chapter 24 of the Book of Exodus describes the solemn ac-ceptance of the covenant by the people. Nevertheless, they quickly prove unfaithful and abandon the worship of Yahweh for the "golden calf." Moses prays on the mountain to turn aside God's anger, and the people are saved from the destruction which they deserve. God gives Moses a glimpse of his glory and proclaims that he is "a God of tenderness and compassion, slow to anger, rich in kindness and faithfulness." The covenant is renewed (chapters 32–34).

The Law

The relationship between God and Israel expressed in the covenant of Sinai was further embodied in the law. God imposed on his people definite obligations toward himself and toward one another. They in turn undertook to keep the law.

The ten commandments contained in chapter 20 of the Book of Exodus are the original form of the law. They are drawn up in the form of a treaty such as a great king in those days would make with his vassals. First, they state the name and title of the sovereign and his claim on the people's allegiance: "I am the Lord your God, who brought you out of the land of Egypt, out of the house of bondage" (Ex 20:2). Then they spell out the chief obligations which the Israelites owed to God (the first three commandments) and to one another (the remaining seven). The last seven commandments were equally part of God's Law with the first three. The prophets later on frequently reminded the people that if they behaved unjustly toward one another they broke the covenant with God just as surely as if they had failed in their duty of divine worship (see, for instance, Is 1:10–17).

The ten commandments were the seed from which grew all the later mass of law material in the Old Testament. As new situations arose, the original brief commands were expanded and adapted. In essence, however, the later legislation simply set out in greater detail what the people were required to do by way of worshiping God and dealing justly with one another. In many points, the legislation in the Pentateuch resembles that to be found in the legal systems of neighboring countries, such as the Code of Hammurabi (a Babylonian king who reigned about 1700 B.C.). As with the stories of creation, so with her laws, Israel was open to borrowing from others. But in both cases, what was borrowed was reshaped by Israel's belief in the one God who had made her his people.

Even those laws which came into being at a much later date were regarded as given by Moses. In fact these later laws were part of the development of a tradition which started with Moses. Often too, they represented a "reform" and an attempt to return to the spirit of the covenant made at Sinai. The earliest of these "developments" comes in the Book of Exodus itself, immediately after the ten commandments (20:22–23:33).

The law continued to be developed down through the ages, both within the written codes of the Bible and in the traditions handed down by the teachers of the law. By the time of our Lord, there was such a mass of laws, both written and unwritten, that there was a serious danger of losing sight of what was really important.

When Jesus was asked which was the greatest commandment of the law, he replied, quoting the Books of Deuteronomy (6:5) and Leviticus (19:18): "You shall love the Lord your God with all your heart, and with all your soul, and with all your mind. This is the greatest and first commandment. And a second is like it: You shall love your neighbor as yourself. On these two commandments depend all the law and the prophets" (Mt 22:34–40). Love of God and of one's fellow human beings goes to the heart of the law, as the prophets had taught in the meantime.

The Holy God: Leviticus

Large sections toward the end of the Book of Exodus (chapters 25–31 and 35–40) are taken up with the building and furnishing of the holy place where God was to be worshiped, with the consecration and the vestments of those who offered worship, and with details of some of the sacrifices. Liturgy is the subject of a great part of the Book of Leviticus, the third book of the Pentateuch and so of the Bible. It describes the divine worship to be carried out by Aaron and the priests descended from him.

Leviticus is inspired by the concern to see the public worship of God carried out correctly, that is, in accordance with God's own will. It lays down exact regulations for animal sacrifices and other offerings, for the consecration of the priests, for ritual cleanliness, and for the celebration of the annual Day of Atonement.

This book is also inspired by a vivid sense of the holiness of God, that is to say, his awesome otherness or apartness. Everything associated with God, including the priests and the place of worship, shared in his holiness and was set aside from ordinary life and dedicated to God alone.

Not only that, but the people whom God had chosen for himself were holy. They were set apart from the other nations and belonged to God. But this carried with it the obligation to live in a way that reflected God's holiness: "And the Lord said to Moses, 'Say to all the congregation of the people of Israel, You shall be holy; for I the Lord your God am holy' " (19:1–2). Chapter 17 to the end of the book consists of the so-called law (or code) of holiness which sets out in detail what it meant to belong to God, in terms both of ritual cleanliness and of moral conduct.

In the Wilderness: Numbers

The Book of Numbers, the fourth book of the Bible, tells the story of the forty years between Israel's exodus from Egypt and the entry into the promised land. (There are also further sections of law interspersed throughout the book.) It was a period of "wandering in the wilderness," although in fact most of the time was spent at the Oasis of Kadesh on the northeastern edge of the Sinai. The forty years are described realistically—the hardships, the people's discontent and lack of faith.

They were also years in which God was close to his people, years to which they looked back later as to a period of first love and courtship (see Hos 2:16–17).

On their journey the Israelites carried with them a wooden chest containing the stone tablets engraved with the ten commandments. This chest, called the ark of the covenant, was regarded as the throne of God on earth. Wherever they encamped, they set up the tabernacle or tent of meeting with God where they worshiped him. Over the tabernacle there hung the shining cloud of God's glory indicating his presence among them.

God cared for his people. When they struck camp, he went before them showing the way with a cloud by day and fire by night. He continued to look after them by giving them food and water. When they had to fight enemies, God was with them in battle—if they trusted him.

The Divine Lover: Deuteronomy

The fifth book of the Pentateuch is Deuteronomy. The name means "second law," and it is a restatement and further development of the law of the covenant, including even a second statement of the ten commandments (chapter 5). The origins of the Book of Deuteronomy appear to be associated with a movement of national reform and renewal originating in the north of the country prior to 721 B.C. and then centered in Jerusalem.

The first thirty chapters of Deuteronomy take the form of speeches made by Moses to the people as they prepare to enter the promised land. He reminds them of their experiences in the wilderness and especially of the covenant which God made with them (chapters 1–11). Then follows a detailed restatement of the law, the so-called Deuteronomic code. This reflects the teachings of the prophets who, during the period of the Israelite monarchy, constantly recalled kings and people to single-hearted service of the true God and tried to purify the national religion of the corruption of idolatry (chapters 12–26). The book ends with Moses' last words (chapters 27–33) and the account of his death within sight of the promised land which he was not allowed to enter (chapter 34).

Throughout the Book of Deuteronomy runs the theme of God's love for his people. It is love which moved God to choose Israel for his own possession. His love is passionate, even jealous—Israel must have no other gods.

The other leading theme is that of the covenant and Israel's obligation to be faithful to it. Acceptance or rejection of the covenant entails momentous consequences for Israel. The people stand at the crossroads with two ways open before them. If they remain true to God and his covenant, he will bless them. They will keep possession of the land God is going to give them, and peace and plenty will be theirs. If not, then they will experience God's curse upon them, and eventually they will be expelled from the land, though not without the possibility of repentance and restoration (see chapters 29–30).

This prophetic insight provides the key for the interpretation of the subsequent history of Israel as expounded in the Books of Joshua, Judges, Samuel and Kings. These books taken together are often called "the Deuteronomist's history" and, as has already been pointed out in chapter 1 of this book, constitute one of the finest achievements of historical writing in ancient times. Far from being mere chronicles, they explain the causes of events which, at the deepest level, are seen to lie in the providential plan of God.

The People of God

All these things and events have a great significance for us Christians. For we have taken part in a new exodus and a new covenant by which God has formed a people for himself, namely the Church.

Before everything else is God's choice of us. "Before the world was made," writes St. Paul to the Ephesians (1:4), God "chose us in Christ." As with his choice of Israel, God's choice of us is not for anything of our own or anything we have done—it is by grace that we have been saved (see Eph 2:8–9).

God has rescued us from the power of Satan, from sin and from death, by the passion and resurrection of his Son. We share in these saving events through the sacrament of baptism. God has made with us a new covenant in the blood of Christ. We celebrate and renew that covenant in the Eucharist, which is both the sacrifice of Christ's body and blood and also a sacred meal in God's presence (compare Exodus 24 and the account of the Last Supper, e.g., Mt 26:20–29). It was at the Last Supper that Jesus gave his "new commandment," the new law of the new covenant, that we should love one another (see Jn 13).

The period of wandering in the wilderness is also instructive for us. For that is where we are now, on a journey from the Egypt of bondage to sin toward the promised land of heaven (see Heb

3–4). We are a pilgrim people. As the Israelites experienced, our journey to the promised land is not by the easiest or shortest route. Most of us will reach our goal by a long and winding way, but as we go along it we are trained and prepared for what awaits us at our destination.

In other respects too, our journey is like that of the children of Israel. At present we also experience hardship and, despite all that God has done for us, we are apt to complain and even to rebel against him. Yet he is patient with us. Even when he punishes us, it is with gentleness, to bring us back to him.

And God is close to us, as he was to Israel in the wilderness. He goes before us, and his presence dwells among us. To sustain us on our journey, he feeds us with bread from heaven—Jesus, who is his living and life-giving word (see Jn 6). And he wins our battles for us—if we trust him.

Even the Book of Leviticus, with its laws governing the Israelite priests and their liturgy, has its interest for us. As the Letter to the Hebrews explains in chapter 9, Jesus is the true and eternal high priest. He has entered the holy place of heaven, of which the tent built by Moses was a copy. He has come right into the presence of God. With him he takes blood to seal the new covenant between God and humankind, not the blood of sacrificial animals, but his own blood shed on the cross. The offering that he makes is once for all. It has the power to take away our sins and make us holy.

For Study or Discussion

1. What is the importance of the exodus for the people of Israel?
2. Read Exodus 24 and Matthew 26:20–29, and point out what they have in common. How does this help our understanding of the Mass?
3. What is a covenant? Is the idea still relevant in Christianity?
4. What place does law have in religion?
5. "The forty years in the wilderness were God's courtship of Israel." What do you think of that statement?

5

The Promised Land

The Land ◊ The Other Nations ◊ Invasion ◊ Struggle for Possession
◊ The Temptations of Paganism ◊ Does This Apply to Us?

The Land

There can be few parts of the world where history has been
more shaped by geography than Palestine. This narrow strip
along the eastern shore of the Mediterranean Sea forms the only
communicating passage, in peace and in war, between the two
ancient centers of civilization in the Near East, namely Egypt to
the south and Mesopotamia to the north.

Palestine was inevitably drawn into the power struggles of
the eastern Mediterranean world. Time and again she has
served as a corridor through which troops passed on their way to
invade an empire. When there was a strong power to north or
south, Palestine was annexed by that power. When a northern
and a southern power fought out their rivalry, Palestine became
their cockpit.

This was the land which God promised to give the descendants of Abraham as their possession.

About 2000 B.C. Palestine and the Syrian coast were part of
the Egyptian empire. However, Egyptian control was growing
weaker, and it was during this period that Abraham and others
like him wandered freely through the region. By about 1400 B.C.
Palestine—or Canaan, as it was then called—was made up of a

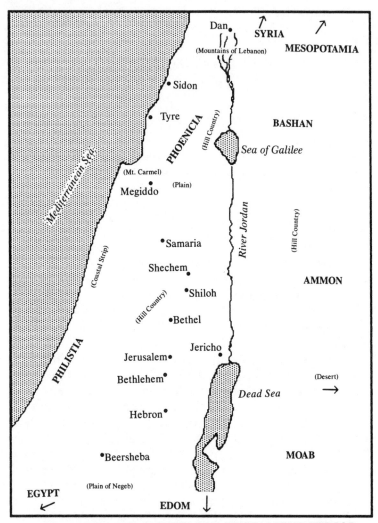

THE HOLY LAND IN THE OLD TESTAMENT PERIOD

number of more or less independent city states under the nominal overlordship of Egypt.

The Canaanite cities were experiencing difficulty in fending off bands of foreigners who were infiltrating into the land, taking what they could for themselves. The Canaanites called these marauders "Habiru" (outlaws). We can easily recognize in this word the name "Hebrews" by which the Israelites came to be known. In fact, when the Israelite tribes, named after the twelve sons of Jacob, began to make their way into the land which God had promised their ancestors, they looked no different from the other Habiru. They even picked up and assimilated other groups of invaders whose origins and experiences were different from their own.

What was the promised land like? It is a strip along the eastern shore of the Mediterranean Sea about seventy kilometers wide. Measured from Dan in the north to Beersheba in the south, it is roughly one hundred and seventy-five kilometers as the crow flies. The land is cleft from north to south by the River Jordan, which rises at the foot of the mountains of Lebanon and then from the Sea of Galilee falls to the Dead Sea at nearly four hundred meters below sea level. In its course the river twists and turns in a valley which in places was a thick jungle where lions once roamed.

On the west side of the Jordan is a high ridge which continues the mountain ranges of Lebanon. This is broken in the northwest by a very fertile plain, then reappears as you go south and finally descends into an arid plateau. Between this ridge and the Mediterranean is a flat coastal area backed by downland which is blocked off toward the north by the ridge of Mount Carmel. To eyes accustomed to the desert, the whole country would appear to be a "land flowing with milk and honey."

The Other Nations

The people of Canaan spoke a language which was closely related to the Hebrew in which most of the Old Testament is written. They were a highly civilized people who had discovered the alphabet—in fact the letters which we use are derived from the ones they invented. They worshiped gods of nature: Baal the life force in the earth, and Astarte the goddess of fertility. Their worship involved orgies and human sacrifices, and God condemned these practices and ordered those who carried them out to be exterminated from the land.

The Israelites had others besides the Canaanites to contend with. To the southeast lay Edom, which was inhabited by a people regarded as being related to the Israelites. To the east of the Dead Sea was Moab, and on the east side of the Jordan was Ammon. Other neighbors were known by various names.

At the same time as the Habiru were penetrating Canaan from the east, other invaders were making their way in from the west, across the Mediterranean Sea. These were the Philistines. Although the Philistines have disappeared, their name lives on in the name "Palestine" which has ever since been applied to the land.

Invasion

The Hebrews under the leadership of Moses had first tried to enter Canaan from the south but were repulsed. They did not have God with them. Eventually, at the end of their wanderings, they conquered territory on the east side of the River Jordan and made that the base for their attack on Canaan.

After Moses died, his place was taken by Joshua, who was destined to lead the people to their goal. The Book of Joshua tells of the conquest of the promised land by the Hebrews and its division among them.

The book falls into three parts. In chapters 1–12, Joshua prepares for the invasion of Canaan, leads the people across the River Jordan as Moses had led them across the Reed Sea, takes the great city of Jericho, and follows up with campaigns in the center, the south and the north of the country. In chapters 13–21, Joshua divides the newly conquered lands among the tribes of Israel. The final chapters, 22–24, narrate the end of Joshua's career, his farewell to the people, and his solemn renewal of the covenant at Shechem.

This last episode is really the climax of the book. God has

shown his faithfulness in giving his people a homeland in accordance with his promises. The people now solemnly reaffirm their allegiance to God.

On reading the Book of Joshua, you get the impression that Canaan was rapidly and completely conquered by the Israelites. Archaeology confirms that there was an important armed invasion at this time, that certain key positions were captured, and that decisive events took place (although not all details of the book—such as the capture of Jericho—can be reconciled with current archaeological data). Under Joshua the Israelites gained territory of strategic importance at the expense of the Canaanites, at the least a foothold from which they were never dislodged and a base from which to expand. But they still had to struggle, even for existence.

Struggle for Possession

This struggle—at times one of life and death—against the Canaanites and also against the Philistines and others is reflected in the next book of the Bible, the Book of Judges. This book also shows that the Israelites established themselves in Canaan not only by outright conquest but also by infiltration and by the assimilation of earlier inhabitants. The Book of Ruth, though written at a much later time, also deals with the period covered by the Book of Judges. (We will discuss the Book of Ruth in Chapter Eight.)

The judges were war leaders raised up by God to rescue his people from their enemies. The material from which the Book of Judges is composed consists of ancient tales of the exploits of these heroes and heroines who saved Israel from destruction. As they are retold in the Bible, some of these episodes are very brief. Others are longer narratives. Of particular interest are the sagas of Deborah and Barak (in both prose and poetry, chapters 4–5), Gideon (chapters 6–8) and—the best known of all—Samson (chapters 13–16).

The period covered by the Book of Judges is one of about one hundred and fifty years, between c. 1200 B.C. and 1050 B.C. Israel is not yet a unified state. Such unity as exists is provided by the common worship of the God of the exodus and the covenant. The individual tribes are establishing themselves in different areas where they come to grips with local enemies.

The judges are not in fact leaders of the whole nation, but only of a single tribe or, at the most, a group of tribes. Cooperation among tribes is rare. All the same there is a slow growth of feeling for national unity. There are signs, however, that the people of Israel are forming into two distinct parts: the north (where all the action of the Book of Judges takes place) under the tribe of Joseph, and the south under the tribe of Judah.

The Temptations of Paganism

During this same period, the Israelites were first exposed to the temptations of the Canaanite religion. In part it was the attraction exerted by a superior civilization and a settled way of life upon newcomers from the desert. As the Hebrews settled down in the land they had won, they naturally adopted the agriculture and many other features of the way of life of the Canaanites. They were inclined also to adopt their religion.

There was a danger that either their faith in Yahweh would be abandoned, or at least that it would be amalgamated with the cult of Baal. Yahweh, however, demanded absolute and exclusive loyalty and even forbade attempts to make images representing him, lest that should lead to confusing him with other gods or to identifying him with his own creatures. Time and again, the Israelites fell into idolatry.

God had a means of bringing his people back to the duty they owed him. He had given them their land in accordance with the covenant he had made with them. If they were unfaithful to the covenant, they were threatened with the loss of their land.

The Book of Judges retells these stories from days gone by in such a way as to form a series of examples of how, as he had said he would in the Book of Deuteronomy, God punishes betrayal of the covenant but comes to the aid of his people when they repent and return to him. Each of the tales of these leaders of olden times shows this pattern. Israel falls away from God. As a punishment, God allows the enemies of the nation to oppress

his people. Israel repents and calls upon God. He raises up a savior, one of the judges. Israel, however, is a slow pupil and soon falls away again.

Does This Apply to Us?

What relevance do these two books, Joshua and Judges, have for us today, and in particular for a Christian reader? The Book of Joshua has traditionally been read in the Christian Church as a foreshadowing of Christ and his saving work. The name Joshua means "Yahweh saves." The Greek form of the same name is Jesus, the name which Joseph was told to give the child who would be born to the Virgin Mary, "because he is the one who is to save the people from their sins" (Mt 1:21). Jesus is our Savior. And just as Joshua led his people into the promised land of Canaan, so Jesus leads his people into the promised land of heaven.

The theme of the Book of Judges has a certain applicability to the situation of the Church and of the individual Christian. We are always in danger of idolatry, of substituting "strange gods" of one sort or another for the true God. If we fall, God may allow us to suffer some setback. But its purpose is to bring us to our senses, so that we will come back to God. If we turn to him once more, he will save us in our affliction.

As St. Paul writes: "All these things happened to them as examples for others, and they were written down as a warning for us. For we live at the time when the end is about to come. Whoever thinks he is standing up had better be careful that he does not fall. Every temptation that has come your way is the kind that normally comes to people. But God keeps his promise, and he will not allow you to be tempted beyond your power to resist; at the time you are tempted he will give you the strength to endure it, and so provide you with a way out" (1 Cor 10:11–13).

For Study or Discussion

1. How does the Book of Joshua show that God is faithful to his promises?

2. Go through the story of one of the judges in the Book of Judges and point out the message it conveys and the way it does so.

3. How was pagan Canaanite religion a temptation to the Israelites?

4. Does the Book of Judges contain a lesson for us?

6

The Kingdom

Foundation ◇ **Rise** ◇ **King David** ◇ **The Books of Samuel** ◇ **Theme: God's Promise to David** ◇ **Glory and Decline** ◇ **The Books of Kings** ◇ **Theme: God's Chastening Hand**

Foundation

During the period of the judges there was a growing feeling that Israel should have a king. Israel would then be like the other nations.

Having a king would also help to weld the nation into unity. Furthermore, the king would command a standing army which could more adequately see to defense. The needs of national defense were very urgent about 1050 B.C. when the Philistines captured the ark of the covenant and threatened Israel with extinction.

The leader of the nation at this time was Samuel who was judge, prophet and priest. He objected to the people's demand for a king. For one thing, Israel was not "like the other nations." Israel already had a king. He was the Lord himself, and a human king would be a usurper. Samuel also pointed out that a king would make heavy demands on the people by way of army service and tribute. Still the people insisted.

Finally God commanded Samuel to give way and provide Israel with a king. Saul was chosen and anointed by Samuel. That was in 1030 B.C. The reign of Saul lasted for twenty years. At first God's favor was with him, and he led the nation to victories against its enemies. However, Saul fell from God's favor because he disobeyed his command. The king of Israel was not to be above the law, but was bound by the covenant as much as any other Israelite.

Rise

Samuel announced to Saul that God had rejected him and then went off to anoint the one who would replace Saul as king. This turned out to be David, the youngest son of Jesse, of Bethlehem in the tribe of Judah.

David was just a boy minding his father's sheep when God called him to be the shepherd of his people. God's choice of David shows a constant feature of his dealings with the human race. Time and time again God chooses the least likely looking people to carry out his designs. As the Lord himself said to Samuel: "God does not see as man sees; man looks at appearances but Yahweh looks at the heart" (1 Sam 16:7).

Under David and his son Solomon, Israel reached her zenith as a political power. These kings justified the hopes which the people had placed in them. The nation was united, secure, and well defended and even able to expand. David defeated the Philistines, who had been such a threat to the Israelites, and conquered Israel's immediate neighbors. At this time too there was no strong power to either the north or the south of Israel, so she was able to exploit her position on the lines of communication between Egypt and Syria, especially the commercial opportunities it gave.

About the year 1000 B.C. David captured the city of Jerusalem from the Canaanite clan which had held it up to then. Jerusalem immediately became the capital. It is a natural strong point and in a central position, on the borders of the tribes of Benjamin (Saul's tribe) and Judah (David's own tribe). Since it had not so far been occupied by the Israelites, it was not identified with any one tribe. Having been taken by the king, Jerusalem was "David's city."

So Jerusalem stood for the royal power and for national unity. It also became the religious center of Israel when David brought the ark of the covenant there and made Jerusalem the chief place of worship. Jerusalem thus became the city of God.

King David

From the Bible we get a vivid impression of the towering personality of King David. He is presented in the round, so that we feel we know the man to a greater extent perhaps than any other Old Testament figure.

He is also presented very frankly. No attempt is made to cover up or gloss over his failings. We are told about David's double sin of adultery and murder and about the punishment which the Lord brought upon him—strife and bloodshed in his own family, leading to revolt and civil war.

However, we learn not only about David's sin, but also about his repentance. King David is one of the great penitents. The "penitential psalms" which bear his name (e.g., Ps 51) are still used by the Church as noble expressions of deep and sincere sorrow for sin.

David's contrition, his deep concern for the worship of God, and his steadfast trust in the Lord in all the ups and downs of life, including extreme danger, justify both Jews and Christians in regarding him as one of the great saints. Like all the saints, he had a deep sense of his own littleness before God.

The Books of Samuel

The events of the reigns of Saul and David are told in the two Books of Samuel (in the Douay Bible, they are called the First and Second Books of Kings). They were originally written as one continuous book.

The First Book of Samuel falls into three parts. Chapters 1–7 describe the judgeship of Samuel and the oppression of the Israelites by the Philistines. Chapters 8–15 tell of the people's demand for a king and of the choice and later the rejection of Saul. Chapters 16–31 are the story of the early life of David, his anointing by Samuel, his famous victory over Goliath, his friendship with Saul's son Jonathan, and Saul's jealousy and persecution of him.

The Second Book of Samuel also falls into three parts. Chapters 1–4 tell how for a few years after the death of Saul in the hour of defeat by the Philistines, David was king over his own tribe of Judah, while the rest of Israel was loyal to Saul's family. Chapters 5–20 are the history of the reign of David over the whole nation, of his victories over the Philistines and other enemies, and of the rebellion of his son Absalom. Chapters 21–24 are a kind of appendix with various documents about King David.

The Books of Samuel draw on many sources, including chronicles, traditions about Samuel and popular accounts of the exploits of David. Some of these sources represent different and even opposing views about, for instance, the value of the monarchy. The most notable source is a continuous narrative which was composed during the reign of David's son Solomon. It is sometimes called the "court history of David" and is a sophisticated account by an eyewitness of the king's private and public life ending with the succession of Solomon.

Theme: God's Promise to David

The Books of Samuel as we have them were written to show that God had established the royal power forever in the house of David. So the climax is the prophecy of Nathan in chapter 7 of the Second Book of Samuel. The Lord promised by the lips of his prophet that David, as a reward for his faithfulness, would have a successor to occupy the throne after him—and not only that: his line would never fail, and there would always be a descendant of David to sit on his throne.

God's promise to David was an unconditional guarantee. It recalls the promise which he made to Abraham, to give him a son and countless descendants. Like that promise, the one made to David was a solemn undertaking on God's part, a covenant. God would never withdraw it. However, he would chastise the son of David if he strayed from the right path, in order to bring him back. In fact, God would treat the king descended from David as his own son.

The promise is celebrated in many of the psalms, notably Psalm 89. It was fulfilled in the first instance when David's son Solomon came to the throne in 970 B.C. Solomon was succeeded by a long line of kings, all descended from David.

God's promise to David reached its final fulfillment in Jesus Christ. He was a descendant of King David, as can be seen from the tables of his ancestry given in Matthew 1 and Luke 4. The angel Gabriel announced to his mother Mary: "The Lord God will give him the throne of his ancestor David; he will rule over the house of Jacob forever and his reign will have no end" (Lk 1:32–33). He was born in Bethlehem, the birthplace of King David, and was hailed as "Son of David" (Mk 10:47–48).

Furthermore, Jesus is the true and only-begotten Son of God. It was strictly only of him that God could say, as he said of David's descendant, "I will be a father to him and he a son to me" (2 Samuel 7:14).

Glory and Decline

The reign of Solomon was truly splendid. Jesus later referred to "Solomon in all his glory" (Mt 6:29). Trade flourished with surrounding countries, and the king established a marriage alliance with Egypt.

It was Solomon who built a magnificent temple for the Lord in Jerusalem. We still have an echo of the temple liturgy in the psalms, many of which were composed to be sung there as part of the worship offered to God.

Other parts of the Bible also have their origin at this time, such as the Wisdom literature, including an important section of the Book of Proverbs (see Chapter Eleven of this book). It was probably at the court of Solomon that the Yahwist version of the national epic was composed (see Chapter Two of this book). It does seem to reflect something of the prosperity, confidence and optimism of this period of Israel's history. (Since the Elohist version now exists only in fragmentary form, it is difficult to say much about it, but many scholars believe it was composed somewhat later in the north of the country.)

After Solomon's death in 931, the nation fell apart. The northern tribes threw off their allegiance to the house of David. They resented the burdens of the monarchy under Solomon, and his successor refused to lighten them. Only Judah (the tribe of David) remained loyal. From that time there were two states—the northern kingdom, called "Israel," and the southern kingdom, called "Judah." Sometimes they fought between themselves, but more often they were at peace, and even in alliance, as they recognized a common religion and nationality.

The Israelite power once divided was weakened. It had to try with increasing difficulty to maintain itself against great powers rising once more in Mesopotamia, and against the struggles of its own vassals to be free.

In 721, the Assyrians conquered the northern kingdom with its capital at Samaria, deported its inhabitants and replaced them with foreign colonists. Judah survived the Assyrian invasion, only to be caught up in the rivalry between Egypt and the Babylonian empire which had succeeded the Assyrian.

Finally, in 587, Jerusalem was taken by the Babylonians under King Nebuchadnezzar. The temple was destroyed, and the king and the leading citizens were taken into captivity. There followed the exile.

The Books of Kings

These events, from the reign of Solomon to the fall of Jerusalem, are told in the two Books of Kings (in the Douay Bible, the Third and Fourth Books of Kings). Like the Books of Samuel, they were originally written as one book.

Taken together, they fall into three main parts. The First Book of Kings, chapters 1–11, covers the reign of Solomon, devoting special attention to the building and dedication of the temple. The rest of the First Book and down to Chapter 17 of the Second Book tells of the division of the kingdom, then gives a parallel history of both north and south to the end of the northern kingdom. The Second Book, chapters 18–27, tells of the last kings of Judah, the fall of Jerusalem and the exile to Babylon.

The Books of Kings were written during the exile by someone who had access to the official records of both kingdoms or at least to chronicles based on them. (These documents are frequently referred to in the course of the narrative.) The "court history of King David" is carried over to the beginning of First Kings. There are also traditions concerning the prophets Elijah and Elisha. All this material has been worked up by an author who surveys the history of the Israelite nation and reflects upon it in the light of the nation's political catastrophe.

Theme: God's Chastening Hand

The disaster posed a real problem for the faith of the Israelites. To all appearances, God has broken his promises, or has not been able to keep them. He had promised his people a land—they are in exile from it. He had promised that David's line would last forever—the king has been deported. Is this the end? Has God been unfaithful? Has he been overcome by the gods of Babylon?

Taking the cue from Deuteronomy, the author of the Books of Kings sees the nation's history as God's judgment on people and kings alike for the way they have not kept the covenant with him. If you look at the past, the writer argues, you will see that time and again the nation and its rulers have broken God's law, especially by their repeated falls into idolatry despite many warnings.

The northern kingdom was especially unfaithful, its beginnings marked by the setting up of images of God at the chief places of worship. But even the southern kingdom, despite having the temple of Jerusalem, was prone to idolatry. Kings Hezekiah and Josiah attempted to bring the nation back to the pure worship of the true God, but each time their successors abandoned their reforms.

So the message of the Books of Kings is that God has not deserted his people, but they have deserted him. They are only getting the punishment which their sins deserve.

Still, God has not cast them off forever. Their punishment is meant to bring them back to him. It is a chastisement, not a rejection. What about the promise made to David and his descendants? God has not repudiated that. He has "corrected" the kings, like a father with wayward sons, as he said he would. But the promise will be fulfilled in the future. How? The answer does not lie within the vision of the author, but the work ends with an account of the reprieve granted to the exiled King Jehoiachin.

The Books of Kings have a lesson for us. Great prosperity blinds us. It makes us get above ourselves and leads us astray. It causes us to forget God. Failure then is the only teacher that can take us in hand again.

For Study or Discussion

1. "King David is one of the great saints." Do you think so?
2. How did God fulfill his promise to David?
3. Try to see the downfall of the kingdom from the point of view of an Israelite at the time.
4. Do the events narrated in the Books of Kings have a lesson for us?

7

A Holy Nation

Return from Exile ◇ Scattered Among the Pagans ◇ Rebuilding the Nation ◇ Chronicles, Ezra and Nehemiah ◇ The True Israel

Return from Exile

After about sixty years, God judged that the exile had had its humbling and purifying effect. From now on the Jewish people would be proof against idolatry. From now on they would be more conscious than ever of their vocation as God's chosen people, set apart for him and marked off from other nations by their observance of the law. They had undergone a conversion, which is movingly described in the Book of Baruch (to be found among the prophetic books).

God therefore allowed his people to return to the land he had given them. Once again his plan was carried out by human agents.

There was another great change in international affairs. In 539 B.C. Cyrus the Great conquered the Babylonians and established the Persian empire. The following year he issued an edict permitting those Jews who wished to do so to return to Jerusalem and rebuild the temple. He allotted state funds to the work.

The prophets described the return from exile in glowing imagery which well expressed its inward significance as a second exodus (see, for instance, Is 49:7–26). The outward appearances, however, were more modest.

The Jews who returned had to overcome many difficulties.

They themselves were few in number—only a minority of the exiles in Babylon took advantage of the edict of Cyrus. They faced the task of rebuilding the city and the temple, which were in ruins, and of starting up the worship of God there once again.

They met with hostility from their neighbors, the Samaritans. These were a mixed population consisting of foreigners who had been settled by the Assyrians in what had once been the northern kingdom and who intermarried with the remnants of the Israelite people there. They worshiped the God of Israel, but the Jews regarded them as unorthodox and would not accept their offer of help in the rebuilding of the temple at Jerusalem. The result was a bitter feud between Jews and Samaritans which persisted for many centuries and is mentioned in the Gospels.

What the returned exiles achieved was on a small scale. The prophet Haggai declared in the name of God that "the new glory of this temple is going to surpass the old." However, those who could remember the old temple wept at the sight of the newly laid foundations of its successor—the contrast was so evident. This second temple, rebuilt by Herod the Great, was to last until its destruction by the Romans in A.D. 70. It was the temple which Jesus knew.

The prophets Haggai and Zechariah also foretold the restoration of the nation under a royal descendant of David. There was at the time a prince of the house of David named Zerubbabel. However, the independent kingdom of Judah was not set up again, and the line of David was destined to sink out of sight. Judea remained a province of the Persian empire, enjoying religious freedom and internal self-government, but was no longer a sovereign state.

Scattered Among the Pagans

As just mentioned, not all of the Jewish exiles returned to their homeland. Many preferred to remain in Babylonia. Many others had taken refuge in Egypt or other places. The result was that, even after the return from exile, there were more Jews living outside Palestine than in the promised land.

These Jews of the dispersion (or "diaspora"), as they were

called, looked to Jerusalem as the center of their religion, paid contributions toward the upkeep of the temple and its liturgy, and made pilgrimages there. It was only to be expected, however, that they should develop a rather distinctive variety of Judaism.

In many respects, the Judaism of the dispersion was more open to Gentiles or non-Jews than was the Judaism of Palestine. This worked both ways. The Jews living among pagans were liable to be influenced by their ideas—sometimes to an extent which other Jews found unacceptable. At the same time, their religion attracted the attention of Gentiles who were looking for a higher understanding of God and a purer morality than was offered by paganism. As a result, Judaism won converts and adherents in many parts of the world.

The Judaism of the dispersion also made its own contribution to the common religion. Greek-speaking Jews in Alexandria, Egypt produced a translation of the Old Testament (called the "Septuagint") and even some books which became part of the Bible (Wisdom, 2 Maccabees).

Rebuilding the Nation

For the Jews who returned to the promised land, the period after the exile was a time of reflection, of rebuilding and consolidation.

For one thing, instructed by the prophets during the exile, they had been able to get their past history into perspective. The written records of the past and of the prophets' teaching had become ever more important to them. An essential aspect of restored Judaism was the recognition of the law of Moses as the binding religious and civil code of the nation and the attempt to build a way of life entirely on the torah.

So it was that this period of Israel's history, which is so lacking in the excitement of great events, was the one in which the Old Testament took shape as we know it. The process of compiling and editing the earlier texts and traditions was completed. The Pentateuch was finished, and the Books of Joshua, Judges, Samuel and Kings reached their final form. It was now also that the collections of the prophets were put together.

Chronicles, Ezra and Nehemiah

As well as fixing the form of the earlier books, post-exilic Judaism produced its own sacred literature. The restored nation wrote the history of its reconstruction and also rewrote the history of the more distant past in terms of its own experiences and values. The realities of national life were, as we have seen, very different from the days of the independent kingdoms. The "new" Jewish nation was centered around the temple, which was its heart, the priests who were its leaders, and the law which was its charter. From now on, religion was uppermost in the life of the nation which, indeed, looked more like a church than a state.

The two Books of Chronicles (called "Paralipomenon" in the Douay Bible) cover the same period of history as the Books of Samuel and Kings. In part they parallel or even reproduce material in the earlier books, but there is also much information in Chronicles not found in Samuel and Kings and apparently obtained from good sources.

However, the perspective of the Books of Chronicles is different. They present a picture of the past which is meant to show that Israel's true vocation was to be literally a nation of priests. This ideal, in the view of the Chronicler, had come closest to fulfillment in the reigns of David and Solomon. But despite the efforts made by some of the kings, the nation as a whole had proved unfaithful to its vocation.

The Chronicler shows a keen interest in the temple and its liturgy, in particular its music. King David is above all the founder of the temple's music and himself a musician and the composer of psalms. On the other hand, his adultery with Bathsheba and the revolt of Absalom are not mentioned.

Chronicles lay, if anything, even greater stress than Kings on the theme of rewards and punishments given by God to rulers and people accordingly as they were faithful or unfaithful to him. They also go further than the earlier books in attributing the course of events—and even the outcome of particular battles—to the direct intervention of God.

The Books of Chronicles have a sequel probably written by the same author, the Books of Ezra and Nehemiah (in the Douay

Bible, the First and Second Books of Esdras) which originally formed a single book. They tell the story of the resettlement of the exiles in Judea and of the rebuilding of Jerusalem and the temple, of the help brought to them by Nehemiah, the high commissioner appointed by the Persian king, and of the religious reforms of Ezra the scribe (who was probably the author of the series Chronicles-Ezra-Nehemiah).

The climax of the restoration comes when Ezra reads out the law (that is, the Pentateuch) to the assembled people. The assembly undertakes to be true to the vocation of Israel to belong to God, embraces his law and celebrates the feast of Tabernacles and the Day of Atonement (see chapters 8–10 of Nehemiah). This event marks the birth of Judaism as a distinct form of religion, in continuity with the religion of Israel before the exile, but with new features and with different emphases.

The True Israel

The Jewish nation at this period saw itself as holy and priestly, in fact "a kingdom of priests, a consecrated nation" (Ex 19:6). This description was eventually applied to the Church (see 1 Pet 2:9).

"Israel" now meant the whole community of God's faithful. It included both the Jews who had returned to Palestine and also the Jews of the dispersion.

But there was a wider prospect still. The community of God's faithful included potentially also the "lost" northern tribes, who would one day be united with Judah. Even the pagans would turn to the true God and be saved (see Isaiah 45). Judaism after the exile, for all that it stressed the separation of Jews from Gentiles, had a universal vision which was to become a reality when Christ broke down the barrier between Jew and non-Jew to make one people of God (see Eph 2:11–22).

For Study or Discussion

1. "In the period after the exile, God was preparing the people for the coming of his Son." How?

2. How did the Jews who returned from the exile see themselves? How did they see their past?

3. What was the diaspora or dispersion? What part did it play in the life of Judaism?

4. How did Judaism after the exile look forward to the Church? Have we anything to learn from it?

Stories with a Message

History, or What? ◇ **Tobit** ◇ **Judith** ◇ **Esther** ◇ **Ruth** ◇ **Jonah**

History, or What?

Judaism after the exile also produced a group of books whose nature is not at all obvious. These are the Books of Tobit, Judith and Esther, which are found together among the historical books after Chronicles, Ezra and Nehemiah; the Book of Ruth, which is found after the Book of Judges; and the Book of Jonah, which is found among the prophetical books. Tobit and Judith, which have come down to us in Greek, are not in some Bibles, or are printed in a separate section called "Apocrypha."

All these books appear to be telling history. However, in reality they are more like historical novels, in which a more or less fictional story is told against the background of real events. In the case of each of these biblical books, the author means to convey some religious or moral message by means of his story. This message is always one that is especially timely for the situation of the Jewish people after the exile and often concerns trust in the providence and protection of God.

Tobit

The Book of Tobit is a romance set among the exiles of the northern kingdom who have been deported to Assyria. Tobit, despite his fidelity to God and his charity toward his fellow exiles, is stricken with blindness. His son Tobias sets out on a journey from the Assyrian capital Nineveh to a distant province of the empire in order to claim as his bride a kinswoman whose previous husbands have all been killed by an evil spirit on their wedding night. He is accompanied on his way by the archangel Raphael in the guise of a young man. Raphael saves Tobias from dangers, helps him overcome the evil spirit and win his wife, and brings him back home with a cure for Tobit's blindness.

This story belongs to the class of those in which a happy ending is snatched from a situation that has all the makings of tragedy. It is a type of literature well suited to a theme which goes right to the heart of the message of the Bible as a whole. As Tobit himself comments, "Blessed be God who lives forever, for his reign endures throughout all ages! By turns he punishes and pardons; he sends men down to the depths of the underworld and draws them up from supreme destruction" (13:1–2). God acts in this way not only toward individuals, but also toward his people as a whole: "Though he punishes you for your iniquities, he will take pity on you all; he will gather you from every nation wherever you have been scattered" (13:5).

Judith

The Book of Judith is also concerned with God's care of Israel. The story tells how God rescued his people from destruction at the hands of an invading army through the agency of a woman. Judith goes to the camp of Holofernes, the enemy general, charms him and wins his confidence, and then, while he is in a drunken stupor, cuts off his head.

This time the story is told against a background which is deliberately fictitious and makes no pretense to be historical. The Book of Judith in fact has a lot in common with those parts of the Bible which look ahead to the last times and to the final victory of God over the united forces of evil arrayed against his saints.

The heroine, whose name means "the Jewess," stands for the nation, so small and defenseless, yet confident in the power of God and able to be used by him as the instrument of his justice. Judith stands also for the many courageous women of Jewish history. The praise which is given to her has also been applied to the Virgin Mary: "You are the glory of Jerusalem! You are the great pride of Israel! You are the highest honor of our race" (15:9–10).

Esther

The Book of Esther, which exists in two versions, a longer version in Greek and a shorter in Hebrew, has for its background the situation of the Jews living in the Persian empire. They are threatened by genocide through the machinations of the grand vizier Haman. Esther, a Jewess, has become the queen of King Ahasuerus (the historical Xerxes). At the prompting of her foster-father Mordecai, she goes to the king and intercedes for her people. The king listens to her and turns his anger against Haman, who is put to death.

The theme of Esther is once again God's protection of his chosen people. This is emphasized in the longer version, which contains Esther's prayer for help and her act of faith and hope in God in chapter 4. Esther's intercession and the foiling of Haman's plot are celebrated by the Jewish people each year on the feast of Purim, when the Book of Esther is read.

Ruth

The idyllic Book of Ruth also has a woman as its central character. Set in the period of the judges, which it faithfully reflects, it is the charming tale of a Moabite woman who married an Israelite. After he died without leaving children, Ruth refused to go back to the land of Moab and remained with her mother-in-law ("Your people shall be my people, and your God my God"—1:16). Her loyalty was rewarded, and she eventually married a kinsman of her first husband by whom she had a son who became the grandfather of King David.

In all likelihood this story with many of its details came down from the time of the events which it relates. However, the Book of Ruth as we have it seems to belong to a much later period, when its message was probably to point out that King David himself was descended from a Gentile woman. It would thus have been intended to counteract tendencies among the Jews after the return from exile to be too exclusive in their dealings with non-Jews and in particular to forbid mixed marriages (compare Ezra 9–10).

Jonah

The Book of Jonah is the story, told with irony and humor, of the reluctant prophet who ran away from God rather than answer his call to preach repentance to the pagan city of Nineveh. Thrown into the sea, Jonah spent three days and three nights in the belly of the sea monster (symbolizing the sea itself, primeval chaos and the underworld) before being vomited up onto the shore. He finally made his way to Nineveh and preached the imminent downfall of the great city. Thereupon its inhabitants did penance, and God spared the city—to Jonah's chagrin.

Jesus made several references to this book in the course of his own ministry. Challenged to produce a "sign," he declared that the only sign that would be given would be "the sign of the prophet Jonah": the release of Jonah from the monster of the deep was a sign of the resurrection of the Son of Man from the dead. And the repentance of the people of Nineveh at the preaching of Jonah condemned the hardness of heart of Jesus' own generation when "there is something greater than Jonah here" (Mt 12:38–41).

The underlying message of the Book of Jonah is a belief in the universal mercy of God, which is not limited to any one group of people but extends to the whole human race and indeed to his entire creation. This appears at the end, when Jonah is angry with God for not destroying Nineveh. God replies: "Am I not to feel sorry for Nineveh the great city, in which there are more than a hundred and twenty thousand people who cannot tell their right hand from their left, to say nothing of all the animals?" (4:11).

For Study or Discussion

1. What are we to make of a book like Tobit, Judith, Esther or Jonah?
2. Take one of the books discussed in this chapter and make a short mime or play of the story. (This could be done also for other books of the Bible.)

9

Persecution, Resistance and Revival

Martyrs and Patriots ◊ **The First Book of Maccabees** ◊ **The Second Book of Maccabees** ◊ **The Hasmoneans and Herod**

Martyrs and Patriots

The Persian empire came to an end about 330 B.C. Its conqueror was Alexander the Great of Macedon. Upon Alexander's death, his vast empire was broken up and parceled out among his generals. Egypt went to one, and Syria and Mesopotamia to another. Palestine thus became once more a contested land between a northern and a southern power. At first it formed part of the Egyptian kingdom, but in 198 B.C. it was annexed by the king of Syria.

The effect of the conquests of Alexander was to spread throughout the Near East the language and culture and also the religion of Greece. Under the rule of the kings of Egypt and Syria, Greek culture reached the Jews of Palestine. Some of them eagerly adopted Greek ways. They were opposed by those who upheld the law of God and the religion of their fathers.

In 167 B.C. King Antiochus IV of Syria decided to impose Greek culture and religion on the Jews by force, in order to unify his dominions. Many Jews went to their death rather than deny their faith. Eventually persecution was answered by revolt, led by the sons of the priest Mattathias, who were known as "the Maccabees" after the nickname of the eldest, Judas Maccabaeus ("the Hammer").

Despite some setbacks, the Maccabees met with success. In 164 the temple was captured and purified from idolatrous worship—an event commemorated each year by the Jewish people on the feast of Hanukkah. Judas fell in battle, but the leadership of what had become a war of national liberation was taken in turn by his brothers Jonathan and Simon. Eventually, the Jews won their independence and even some international importance.

The First Book of Maccabees

The story of the Maccabean War is told in the Books of Maccabees, which are not included in some Bibles or are classed as "Apocrypha." First Maccabees was written about 100 B.C. in Hebrew but survives only in a Greek translation. It is modeled not only on earlier biblical history but also on the historical writings of the ancient Greeks. (Notice the extent of Greek cultural influence even among religious and patriotic Jews in Palestine where the book was composed.) Like the Greek historians, the author describes battles, political intrigues, and diplomatic missions, reports speeches and reproduces documents.

However, 1 Maccabees is still in the tradition of biblical history, seeing the events in fundamentally religious terms. Its heroes are fighting not just for national independence, but for the survival of the Jewish religion and faith in the true God. Like earlier writers, this author sees the reverses suffered by the nation as due to sin, and its successes as due to the power of God. Throughout the whole book, there appears a firm belief in divine providence guiding the course of events.

Chapter 1 of 1 Maccabees describes the infiltrations of paganism and the outbreak of persecution culminating in the desecration of the temple. In chapter 2 Mattathias raises the revolt. Chapters 3–9 narrate the career of Judas Maccabaeus, the high point of which is the rededication of the temple (4:36–61). Judas' brother Jonathan wins concessions from the kings of Syria and Egypt, including the title of high priest for himself (chapters 10–12). The independence of the Jewish nation is now guaranteed by Sparta and Rome, and the third brother Simon is able to consolidate the gains of Judas and Jonathan and his own position as ruler, until he is treacherously killed in 134 B.C. (chapters 13–16).

The Second Book of Maccabees

The Second Book of Maccabees is not, as its title seems to suggest, a continuation of the First Book. It is a completely independent work by a different author writing in Greek and modeling himself on certain types of Greek literature much read in those days. (In fact, the book as we have it describes itself as a condensation of a longer work written by a certain Jason of Cyrene.)

The period covered by 2 Maccabees ends before the death of Judas. For that period, the book fills out the picture given by 1 Maccabees. The two books overlap to some extent, but 2 Maccabees also supplies a certain amount of information which is not in the other. It is, for instance, much clearer in 2 Maccabees that a large party of Jews went along willingly, even enthusiastically, with the introduction of Greek customs and ideas.

However, the tone and the approach of 2 Maccabees are quite different. The purpose of the author is to arouse the sympathy of the Jews of Alexandria for the struggles of their brethren in the holy land. He is especially interested in the temple as the center of Judaism and as the object of pagan hatred. In 2 Maccabees divine intervention is more obvious and is frequently accompanied by heavenly apparitions.

The Second Book of Maccabees contains much clearer teachings about life after death than are to be found in other books of the Old Testament. The dead are to rise again. There are rewards and punishments in the afterlife. For those still in this life, it is a "fine and noble action" to pray and offer sacrifice for the departed, "that they might be released from their sins" (12:38–45). The saints, such as Jeremiah, make intercession before God for the living and can help them (15:15–16). Those who die a martyr's death for their faith merit eternal life. The value of martyrdom is movingly taught in the stories of Eleazar (6:18–31) and of the seven brothers (7:1–42).

The Hasmoneans and Herod

Simon left a son John who succeeded him and thus founded a dynasty of rulers known as the Hasmoneans (from the name of an ancestor of the clan). They eventually assumed the title of king.

For a while the Hasmoneans pushed back the frontiers of the Jewish state over a much wider territory than that possessed by the old subject province of Judaea. Transjordania was conquered. In Idumaea (Edom) to the south, and Galilee to the north, their pagan inhabitants were converted, and Jewish settlements were planted. Samaria was taken and its heretical temple on Mount Garizim was destroyed. It seemed that the great days of David and Solomon had returned.

Meanwhile the power of Rome had been growing and eventually began to be felt in the eastern Mediterranean. In 64 B.C. Pompey the Great made Syria a Roman province. In the following year he visited Jerusalem and showed the Jews that Rome was now mistress of the world.

The Hasmoneans quarreled among themselves, and their power declined. During the shadowy reigns of the last of the dynasty, the real ruler of Judaea was the minister Antipater, a foreigner (from Idumaea). Eventually, in 37 B.C. Antipater's son Herod was made king with the help of his Roman friend Octavian who became the Emperor Augustus.

Herod's reign until 4 B.C., though bloodstained, was in many ways brilliant, as his magnificent buildings still testify. His grandest project was the rebuilding of the temple, which he did not live to complete. He also built the port and city of Caesarea, and a number of palaces and fortresses, including the famous stronghold of Massada on the Dead Sea.

Herod is known to history as "the Great." In reality, however, Judaea was a client kingdom dependent on Rome. The Jewish nation had once again lost its political independence.

Neither Herod nor the Hasmoneans were descendants of King David. That line was now represented by obscure individuals like Joseph the carpenter.

For Study or Discussion

1. "The two Books of Maccabees show two different responses to persecution: resistance by force and martyrdom." Look again at both books in the light of this analysis.
2. In what ways were the Jews put to death by Antiochus the forerunners of the early Christian martyrs?

10

Singing to the Lord

Poetry in the Bible ◇ Hebrew Poetry ◇ The Book of Psalms ◇ Types of Psalms ◇ Praying the Psalms

Poetry in the Bible

The Book of Psalms (or Psalter) occupies a central position in the Bible, in every sense of that phrase. It is a collection of one hundred and fifty religious poems, many of them addressed directly to God. Nearly all of them are quite short.

Poetry is found in other parts of the Bible as well, notably in the wisdom books and in the prophets. Its origins are to be sought in popular and traditional songs of work, love, war, lamentation and worship. Some of these songs are included in the Bible, for example the song of triumph of the Israelite women over the Egyptians (Ex 15:21).

More sophisticated poetry was developed from these songs, often under the influence of the literature of neighboring cultures, Egyptian, Mesopotamian, and especially Canaanite. The Bible contains examples of poems composed in very ancient times, such as the epic song of Deborah and Barak (Jgs 5), which dates from about 1100 B.C., and the lament of David over Saul and Jonathan (2 Samuel 1:19–27), which dates from 1010 B.C. It is worth remembering that, even in its developed literary forms, Hebrew poetry, especially in lyrics such as the psalms, never lost its connection with music.

Hebrew Poetry

In Hebrew literature, as in English, poetry differs from prose by its greater use of imagery and figures of speech, such as metaphor and personification, e.g. "You (God) are my rock, my fortress" (Ps 71:3) and "Righteousness and peace now embrace" (Ps 85:10). The difference is also marked by the use of a regular rhythm or beat and by the choice of words whose sounds chime together.

The rhythm of Hebrew poetry is like a pulse running through the line. Each line may have a different number of syllables in it, but it will have a regular number of beats, two, three, or four. Certain rhythms were associated with particular types of poetry, such as the lament, in which a three-beat line is paired with a two-beat line (the silent third beat in the second line is like a sigh, and its effect is to intensify the emotional impact).

The sound patterns in Hebrew poetry are not exactly the same as in English verse. There is no rhyme (or hardly any). There is, however, assonance, that is, the placing together of words with similar sounds, e.g. Shakespeare's "Full many a glorious morning have I seen," and alliteration, when several words begin with the same sound, e.g., "When to the sessions of sweet silent thought." A number of Hebrew poems, including several psalms, are written in such a way that the first word of each verse begins with the successive letters of the alphabet, e.g., Psalm 119 and Proverbs 31:10–31.

The most distinctive feature of Hebrew poetry is what is called "parallelism." It seems instinctively to arrange things in pairs. Often words come in pairs ("mercy and faithfulness," "the poor and needy"). The lines of verse also are paired, with the second line matching the first.

Sometimes the second line echoes the first, as in:

Be pleased, O God, to deliver me!
O Lord, make haste to help me (Ps 70:1).

Sometimes the second line is in contrast to the first, as in:

But I am afflicted and in pain;
let thy salvation, O God, set me on high (Ps 69:29).

At other times the second line continues the thought of the first, as in:

In his days may righteousness flourish,
and peace abound, till the moon be no more (Ps 72:7).

The effect of this parallelism is not unlike that of Oriental music (such as the psalms were written to be sung to) which never moves far from its themes but constantly repeats them with endless variations.

Each poem is made up of one or several sets of these pairs of lines. Most modern editions of the Bible print the psalms and other poetry in such a way that their verse structure is immediately obvious, with the English translation matching as far as possible the rhythm, pairing of lines and arrangement of stanzas of the Hebrew original.

The Book of Psalms

The Book of Psalms as we have it is a collection of earlier collections. It is now divided into five "books" (no doubt in imitation of the Pentateuch, the five books of Moses), with Psalm 1 as an introduction and Psalm 150 as a conclusion to the entire collection. But the titles of many of the psalms indicate that they were once grouped in series, such as those that are named after the various choirs in the temple ("the sons of Korah" and "the sons of Asaph") or the "songs of ascents" (? pilgrim songs), Psalms 120–134.

The editing of the collection is not perfect (by modern standards). Some poems appear twice—compare Psalm 108 with Psalm 57:7–11 and Psalm 60:5–12. Sometimes one poem is artificially separated into two psalms, and the reverse can also happen, with two originally separate poems being combined. This is the explanation of the different numbering systems for the psalms, which can cause confusion. Psalms 9 and 10 were written as one poem, but they are divided in the Hebrew Bible and in those translations which follow it (King James, Revised Standard, etc., and also the Jerusalem Bible). The Greek and Latin translations used by the early Church preserved the original unity of this psalm, as do most translations made under Catholic auspices. Hence, throughout most of the Psalter there is a discrepancy in the numbering between various editions of the Bible, so that, for instance, the well-known psalm "The Lord is my shepherd" is Psalm 23 in some and Psalm 22 in others.

Tradition ascribes the origins of Israel's religious poetry to King David and credits him with the authorship of many of the psalms. The Bible in fact has a great deal to say about David's concern for worship and about his abilities as a musician and a singer (see 2 Samuel and 1 Chronicles). Two series of psalms (Pss 3–41 and 51–70), as well as some further on in the Psalter, bear the title "of David."

On the other hand, the historical notes in many of the psalm titles saying that a particular psalm was composed by David on such or such an occasion are not necessarily reliable. Also, the psalms as we have them, even those which originated with David, may have been considerably changed after his time. Finally, in the New Testament (and presumably in the Jewish world of the time) "David" has become another name for the Book of Psalms, like "Moses" for the Pentateuch or "Solomon" for the wisdom books, so that a quotation from "David" should not be taken as a claim that the psalm in question was actually composed by him.

Religious poetry continued to flourish in Israel under David's successors, and it seems that the period of the monarchy before the exile was the great age of the psalms. The earliest poems of this type would have been composed for the liturgy in Jerusalem, which David made the religious as well as the political capital of the nation, and also to express personal religious feelings. These two concerns—the public worship of God and the expression of religious experience—remained central to the tradition and run right through the Psalter.

Types of Psalms

Many of the psalms were composed for the temple liturgy or were adapted to it. The text of a number of them even contains musical directions for their performance, such as the name of the tune to which they were to be sung ("Lilies" or "Doe of the Dawn"

or "Do Not Destroy"), or the instruments to accompany the singing, or the direction "Selah," which probably means "instrumen-
tal interlude." Other psalms appear to have originated in private
poems, but at some stage they, too, found a place in public worship, as other individuals made use of them for their own needs
or the community identified itself with the thoughts and feelings
of the poet.

A great number of psalms are hymns of praise to God, e.g.
Psalms 145–150. These begin with a call to praise God and dwell
on the motives of praise, either the wonders of creation or God's
mighty deeds of salvation.

Another group are psalms of petition. These are addressed directly to God and come out of situations of distress. They are cries
for help to the God who saves. Some of these psalms voice the suffering of the whole nation in an emergency or after a catastrophe,
e.g., Psalm 44, or Psalm 74 which is a lament on the destruction
of the temple. Other psalms of this type are cries from the heart
of individuals who are in the grip of sickness (Pss 38, 41, 88), personal enemies (Pss 3, 6, 22), or sin (Pss 51, 130). Psalms of en-
treaty usually end on a note of confidence in God.

Thanksgiving is the occasion of a further group of psalms. In
them either the nation as a whole or a single individual gives
thanks to God for help in time of danger or distress. Examples are
Psalms 18, 30, 65–68, 116, and 118.

Other types of psalms can be identified. There are, for instance, the "royal psalms," first composed to celebrate royal occasions, such as a victory (Ps 21) or a wedding (Ps 45), or to pray
for the welfare of the king (Ps 20). After the exile, when the descendants of David were not restored to the throne, these psalms
continued to be used. It seems, however, that they were now seen
as expressing the Jews' expectation of the Messiah (see Chapter
Twelve). Some appear to have been rewritten in order to bring out
more clearly their Messianic meaning, notably Psalm 2 and Psalm
110.

This illustrates something that went on with many of the
psalms. A good number of them originated during the period of
the monarchy. So they were sung and prayed continuously for
hundreds of years before Christ. As people prayed the psalms,

they applied them to new situations which were not, of course, envisaged by those who composed them, and saw new meanings in them. Some of these new meanings were suggested by a deepened understanding of the faith and religion of Israel, or by the rise of new doctrines, such as the resurrection of the dead. Often the older psalms were reworked to adapt them to the later setting. Alternatively, the traditional words were still employed but were now understood in a more spiritual way, so that, for instance, "salvation," which had meant being rescued from physical enemies, now meant being rescued from spiritual enemies, such as sin or the devil.

Eventually the whole Psalter was caught up in the movement of the Bible which looked forward to a coming fulfillment. In one way or another, more or less openly and directly, everything in the psalms came to be seen as referring to the decisive intervention of God in the world and to the Messiah who would bring it in. David the singer became also David the prophet.

Praying the Psalms

The psalms have been used in public and private prayer for thousands of years down to the present day, by both Jews and Christians. On one level this is a tribute to their success as poetry. How many other collections of lyric poems—Shakespeare's sonnets, for instance, or, perhaps better, an anthology such as Palgrave's *Golden Treasury*—could stand up to such constant and repeated use by so many people? The success of the psalms as poetry lies in the range of their subject matter and of the emotions expressed, in their vigorous language and vivid imagery, and in their economy with words, all of which comes across even in translation.

But, of course, the vast majority of people who have read or recited the psalms have used them as prayers. They have sung them in a choir, said them out loud to themselves, or meditated on them line by line. It is as prayers that the psalms need to succeed.

For the individual person at private prayer, the Psalter is a rich resource book. It is possible to find a psalm for every situation and every emotion. The whole spectrum of religious experience is there, from the "dark night of the soul" (Ps 88) to mystical desire for God (Ps 63), from doubt to radiant confidence (both in Ps 73). Many people have found that one of the best ways of developing a deep and full prayer life based on the Scriptures and in touch with the liturgy has been to grow familiar with the psalms, to enter into the prayer which they voice, to dwell on their ideas and images, and to store up phrases of the psalms in the memory. The use of the psalms in the liturgy of the word at Mass has helped Catholics get to know them better.

However, people can experience difficulties in praying with the psalms, both in public and in private use. Some of these difficulties may disappear if we bear in mind that the psalms are poems and even songs. They are not meant to be read as plain, matter-of-fact statements. In fact they were not meant to read at all, at least not silently to oneself. They were originally composed to be chanted and sung out loud, to the accompaniment of musical instruments or even dancing. So it is not surprising to experience the psalms "come alive" for the first time when one hears them sung to music. Even in private prayer, one may get more out of the psalms by singing them to oneself. Realizing that the psalms are poetry, one will expect them to abound in striking images which cannot be taken literally, in deliberate exaggerations for effect, in vehement expressions of strong emotions.

One particular type of psalm is apt to upset modern people, and that is the cursing psalm, which expresses the hope that enemies will come to a violent end, their children orphaned and dispossessed, and so forth, e.g., Psalm 109. How can we make such prayers our own? The problem is felt to be so great that modern editions of the psalms for use as prayer tend to leave out the curses. They do, however, honestly express a genuine human emotion—not an emotion that one is proud of, it is true, but an emotion that anybody is liable to experience. Who has not on occasion felt bitter hostility, or the desire for revenge, or satisfaction at someone else's discomfiture? If so, then one will find that feeling, too, reflected in the psalms.

It is a different matter, of course, to make such feelings part of our own prayer. We are, after all, supposed to love our enemies and pray for those who persecute us (see Mt 5:44). One traditional solution is to direct the curses of the psalms against "the enemy of the human race," Satan, and all the powers of darkness.

The psalms share with other parts of the Bible the difficulty that we cannot now enter exactly into all the thoughts and feelings of the original composers and their first hearers. This difficulty is more likely to be felt in the case of the psalms because of the use made of them in prayer. What, for example, are we to make of:

> I will pay my vows to the Lord
> in the presence of all his people,
> in the courts of the house of the Lord,
> in your midst, O Jerusalem (Ps 116:18–19)?

When it was first written, there was a temple in Jerusalem, and it was the intention of the psalmist to go there and offer sacrifice. There is no longer a temple in Jerusalem, and no sacrifices.

We are really in no different a situation from that of the Jews who continued to use the royal psalms after the end of the monarchy. We too will need to see if the psalm is applicable in any way to our situation, and so find new possibilities of meaning in it. Notice that we would be doing this even if we chose to make the words from Psalm 116 a prayer for the restoration of the Jerusalem temple, even if we used them to mean that we intended to make a pilgrimage to Jerusalem and pray at the site of the former temple.

In the ongoing life and worship of the Christian Church, references to the temple have been applied to Christ who is himself the meeting place between God and humankind, to the Church which is his body, to the individual Christian who is the temple of God and of the Holy Spirit, and to heaven where God dwells. So in praying those lines of Psalm 116, one could have in mind Christ and his perfect worship of the Father continued in the Church and its liturgy, or one's own heart where one can offer intimate prayer to God, or heaven where one hopes to praise him forever.

For Study or Discussion

1. What is the best way to approach the psalms in order to appreciate them?
2. How can we pray the psalms?
3. What aspects of God are conveyed by the psalms?

11

The Wisdom of Israel

Wisdom Writing ◇ The Scribes ◇ Wisdom in Israel ◇ Job ◇ Proverbs ◇ Ecclesiastes ◇ The Song of Songs ◇ The Book of Wisdom ◇ Ecclesiasticus ◇ The Wisdom of God

Wisdom Writing

Around the middle of the Bible comes a group of books known collectively as "the wisdom books." They are the Books of Job, Proverbs, Ecclesiastes, The Song of Songs, Wisdom and Ecclesiasticus. The last two are not found in some Bibles, or they may be printed separately as "Apocrypha." The Psalms actually come between Job and Proverbs, but they are not really "wisdom literature," and we have seen them on their own in Chapter Ten of this book.

"Wisdom" is a type of writing found in many places in the Bible. Some of the psalms, e.g., Psalm 49, could be called "wisdom psalms," and the story of Joseph in the Book of Genesis appears to be the product of the "wisdom" tradition, as are also the Books of Tobit and Baruch. There are even traces of the "wisdom" style in the New Testament, e.g., in the Letter of James.

The wisdom books have left their mark on later literature too. Parts of the *Imitation of Christ* read remarkably like sections of the Books of Proverbs and Ecclesiasticus. "Man proposes, God disposes," perhaps the best known saying of the *Imitation,* has a close parallel in Proverbs 16:1.

"Wisdom" was in fact a type of literature found all over the ancient Near East. We possess wisdom writings from Egypt and Syria, and the sages of these and other nations are quoted and referred to in the Bible itself.

These sages of the East made it their business to pass on advice about how to live well. On the whole, by "well" they meant "successfully." They composed and handed down their instructions in the form of pithy, striking statements and sayings which were easily memorized. As the wisdom tradition developed, these brief remarks tended to expand into various longer forms, such as the parable, of which Jesus made such effective use in his own teaching.

The Scribes

Good advice has, of course, been given at all times by some people to others. But the sort of good advice which formed the wisdom tradition was cultivated by the "scribes." They were a class of professional writers who passed on their skills to their pupils in regular schools. At the same time, they handed on their experience of life, their observations and reflections about people and things.

It was from this class that rulers drew their officials and administrators. So we find that many wisdom sayings are about how to "get on" at the courts of kings and among the great ones of this world. Other wisdom sayings reflect rather traditional "folk wisdom," the accumulated store of experience and reflection down through the generations.

Wisdom writing came to Israel with the establishment of the centralized monarchy under David and Solomon. The Israelite kings modeled their government on that of neighboring countries and looked there also to find qualified officials to staff their own administration and to train up local people. The scribes of Egypt and Syria brought with them their own tradition of "wisdom" and transplanted it to Israel, where it flourished for many centuries. The Hebrew scribes eventually came to be grouped with the teachers of the law, and it is as such that we meet them in the New Testament.

Wisdom in Israel

The wisdom tradition in Israel regarded its founder as King Solomon. He had the reputation of being the wisest man in Israel and indeed in the whole world. Much of what we are told about him in the Bible has to do with his wisdom: his prayer for wisdom and his famous judgment between two women who claimed the same baby (1 Kgs 3), his encyclopedic knowledge (1 Kgs 5:9–14), the visit of the queen of Sheba to hear his wisdom for herself (1 Kgs 10:1–13). No one wiser than Solomon arose in Israel until, many centuries later, his own descendant was able to claim: "There is something greater than Solomon here" (Mt 12:42).

The Books of Proverbs, Ecclesiastes and Wisdom bear the name of King Solomon, as does also the Song of Songs. This device of attributing a book to some great personage of the past (it is often called "pseudepigraphy") gave the book authority and assured it of an audience. However, it was not done with a dishonest intention. In the case of the wisdom books named after Solomon, they did in fact come out of a tradition which began with Solomon and was always closely associated with him.

Since "wisdom" came to Israel from other nations, it is not surprising that a great deal of the wisdom literature in the Bible closely resembles the wisdom writing of other lands. This explains why many of the sayings to be found there do not appear to be very religious. Some indeed strike us as decidedly worldly wisdom.

However, as the wisdom tradition developed in Israel, wisdom was seen more and more in terms of the religion of Yahweh. "Living well"—the subject of all wisdom writing—came to mean unmistakably "living a good life." "Wisdom" meant "virtue," and its opposite, "foolishness," meant "vice." In the last analysis, both "wisdom" and "virtue" amounted to "true religion." Eventually, the sages could say, "The fear of Yahweh is the beginning of wisdom" (see, for instance, Prov 9:10 and Ps 111:10).

For all that, the wisdom tradition was marked by a certain breadth of view and even universalism. God's revelation was seen as not restricted to Israel, since wisdom could be attained and appreciated by the sages of all nations, and wisdom came from God and led to God. The wisdom books of the Bible in effect presented an ethic of right conduct which is available to all, not only to Jews but also to those who do not share in Israel's sacred history and the law revealed to Moses.

Job

The Book of Job, written between 500 and 400 B.C., is one of the masterpieces of the Bible. It takes as its basis a traditional story of the sufferings and patience of Job, who was supposed to have lived in the East about the time of Abraham and to have worshiped the one true God. The story of Job is told in the prose prologue and epilogue, which are set in heaven and on earth. The body of the book, however, consists of a series of speeches written in poetry and is therefore a sort of epic drama.

The writer of the Book of Job sets out in terms of this proverbial figure of patience a sublime and powerful discussion of the problem of evil or suffering. This was in fact the great problem which the sages of Israel wrestled with and which they returned to again and again. It is for that matter a problem which still troubles us today.

The God of Israel was a God of morality. His people could not conceive of him except as a just God who loves justice. He made moral demands on them and would reward or punish them in accordance with their deeds.

So it was with extreme anguish that they put the question: Why then do the innocent suffer while the wicked prosper? Because that—despite the assurances of some passages in the Old Testament to the contrary—is what happens in this world. And this world was where, for most of the Old Testament period, it was taken for granted that God's rewards and punishments had to be dealt out. After death there would be only the twilight existence of the underworld to which all alike—good and bad, high and low, wise and foolish—must come. So how could a just God allow the innocent to suffer and the wicked to prosper?

In our book, Job suffers atrociously. Conscious of his innocence, he challenges God to explain why he has treated him as he has. Three friends ("Job's comforters") supply the stock answer:

if Job suffers, it is because he has sinned. Job will have none of it and persists with his agonized questioning. God finally appears and rebukes his three advocates. But still no answer is given to Job, except that God is not answerable to human beings, who must surrender themselves to God. Job's last words to God are: "I had heard of thee by the hearing of the ear, but now my eye sees thee; therefore I despise myself and repent in dust and ashes" (Job 42:5–6).

When God eventually did answer Job, it was on the cross. In the meantime, one of the great saints of the Old Testament had seen the possibility of suffering on behalf of others and carrying the burden of their sins (see Is 52:13–53:12).

Proverbs

The Book of Proverbs is the basic work in the series. Its central section consists of several collections of brief sayings which date in the main from the period of the monarchy. Two of these collections (chapters 10–22:16 and chapters 25–29) are attributed to Solomon himself. The book ends with a poem in praise of the perfect wife (31:10–31) which is read in the Jewish family liturgy every Sabbath eve (Friday evening).

In addition to containing a great deal of secular wisdom, the Book of Proverbs preserves many sayings which convey a truly religious outlook and teach a practical morality. This book is frequently quoted or referred to in the New Testament. The Beatitudes, as well as many other passages in Jesus' Sermon on the Mount, contain echoes of its teaching. Thus "Happy the gentle: they shall have the earth for their heritage" (Mt 5:4) recalls "For the land will be for honest men to live in, the innocent will have it for their home" (Prov 2:21), and "Happy those who hunger and thirst for what is right: they shall be satisfied" (Mt 5:6) is in the tradition of "He who pursues virtue and kindness shall find life, justice, and honor too" (Prov 21:21).

The first nine chapters of the Book of Proverbs date from after the exile. They sing the praises of Wisdom and tell how she is to be acquired. These chapters in fact illustrate a remarkable development which took place in the wisdom tradition. The sages saw that their wisdom came from God. Wisdom properly belongs to God, who alone is truly wise.

Eventually the wisdom writings tended to portray Wisdom as a person, who is with God and yet distinct from him, who aids him in the creation and government of the universe and whose delight is to be with human beings (see Prov 8:22–31).

Ecclesiastes

The Book of Ecclesiastes or Qoheleth ("the Preacher" or "Speaker") probably dates from the third century B.C. and shows the influence of new currents of thought from abroad, including Greece. It is a set of variations on a theme: the emptiness of all things human and created. "Vanity of vanities! All is vanity" (1:2).

The writer reviews in turn all the things that might be thought to make people happy—knowledge, pleasure, wealth. He has experienced everything and is oppressed by the thought that there is nothing new under the sun. Everything is "vanity" because everything comes to an end with death. His mind goes to and fro restlessly. He can find no lasting fulfillment in this world, and yet does not know where else it might be found. He is not convinced that there is life after death, at least any that would be worth living. His final mood is one of resignation as he concludes: "Fear God and keep his commandments, since this is the whole duty of man" (11:13).

Some readers feel that the disillusioned tone and relentless questioning of Ecclesiastes is out of place in the Bible. However, it is fitting that all human experience should be reflected there, even world-weariness and doubt. Furthermore, Ecclesiastes ruthlessly exposes the insufficiency of created things to satisfy the craving of the human heart.

The Song of Songs

The Song of Songs (i.e., "the greatest song of all"), which dates from the fifth century B.C., is a series of love poems or songs exchanged between a bride and bridegroom with occasional lines for a chorus. The setting changes constantly between a country village and a royal court, with the hint of a still deeper level of meaning.

The literary background to this work appears to be a tradition of pastoral poetry not unlike the Eclogues of Vergil and certain poems of Shakespeare and Milton. The rustic love songs of real-life shepherds and shepherdesses have been adapted to the more sophisticated ideas and polished expressions of elegant lords and ladies. Throughout the series, the bridegroom is frequently identified as King Solomon, and the poems have absorbed the imagery of a royal wedding (as in Ps 45), perhaps with historical memories of the marriage of Solomon with the daughter of Pharaoh (see 1 Kgs 3:1).

There is no reason, of course, why human love and marriage should not be the subject of a book of the Bible. In fact, however, tradition, both Jewish and Christian, has constantly seen these themes in the Song as symbolizing divine love (as in the commentaries of several Fathers of the Church and the *Spiritual Canticle* of St. John of the Cross which is based on the Song). Such a symbolism is not foreign to the Bible, where the love of a husband for his wife is frequently used by the prophets as an image of the love of God for his people, sealed in the marriage bond of the covenant.

Many different interpretations of the Song of Songs have been put forward. It seems, however, that its love poems and wedding songs are intended to look forward to the coming of the Messiah, who is symbolized by the bridegroom–King Solomon. They celebrate in anticipation the union of the Messiah with Israel, symbolized by the bride. St. Paul continues this line of thought in Ephesians 5:21–33, when he compares the love of Christ, i.e., the Messiah, for his Church to the love of a husband for his wife.

It is of great interest that in this passage Paul quotes Genesis 2:24, "For this reason, a man must leave his father and mother and be joined to his wife, and the two will become one body," and comments: "This mystery has many implications, but I am saying it applies to Christ and his Church." The link between the Song of Songs and Paul runs back to the beginning of the Bible, where, as we have seen, one of the great originating symbols is that of the man and the woman, the bridegroom and the bride. The same link runs ahead to the end of the Bible, the Book of Revelation, which rejoices in the marriage of the Lamb (19:5–9) and describes "the new Jerusalem, coming down from God out of heaven, as beautiful as a bride all dressed for her husband" (21:2).

The Song of Songs can be read as the pivotal book of the Bible, devoted as it is to a theme which runs right through the Bible and expresses its central message. This celebration of the love of man and woman in a world which has become their playground is the depiction of paradise regained, as the bridegroom goes down to his garden and awakens his beloved under the apple tree (see 6:2 and 8:5).

The Book of Wisdom

The Book of Wisdom, the last Old Testament book to be written, was probably composed in Alexandria about 50 B.C. by a Greek-speaking Jew. It is designed to bolster up the faith of Jews living in the midst of pagans and also to attract pagan readers to Judaism.

Chapters 1–5 once again discuss the great question of the suffering of the innocent. Now, however, an answer can be given in terms of the immortality of the soul, an idea which shows the influence of Greek thought. Whatever the experiences of this life, God will reward the good and punish the wicked in the next life. It is after death that his justice will be seen to be done. Meanwhile we can be confident that "the souls of the virtuous are in the hands of God" (3:1).

Chapters 6–9 also deal with a traditional theme: the origin and nature of wisdom and how it is to be acquired. King Solomon is speaking, and in chapter 9 he utters a beautiful prayer for wisdom which is a developed version of his prayer as given in 1 Kings 3:6–9. This section of the book is the fullest reflection on wisdom in the Old Testament. The description of Wisdom as "the untarnished mirror of God's active power, image of his goodness" (7:28) was taken up by St. Paul and applied to Christ who is "the image of the unseen God" (Col 1:15).

Chapters 10–19 are a reflection on the history of Israel, dwelling especially on the exodus. (We recall that this book was written in Egypt.) The accounts of the ten plagues and the crossing of the Reed Sea given in the Book of Exodus are developed at some length. The author throws light on the action of God in which both justice and mercy are displayed and contrasts the wisdom of the Israelites with the folly of the idolatrous Egyptians. "Yes, naturally stupid are all men who have not known God and who, from the good things that are seen, have not been able to discover him-who-is" (13:1)—a thought taken up by St. Paul in Romans 1:19–20.

Ecclesiasticus

The Book of Ecclesiasticus or "The Wisdom of Jesus Ben Sirach" was written in Hebrew in Palestine and, as its preface tells us, was translated into Greek in Alexandria by the author's grandson in 132 B.C. for the benefit of the Jews of the dispersion. It went through several editions, both in Hebrew and Greek, resulting in marked differences among the various texts which have come down to us.

A great deal of the material in Ecclesiasticus is of the traditional wisdom type. However, there are new features. Ben Sirach shows great veneration for the temple and its liturgy and priests, as well as zeal for the law. In fact he identifies wisdom and torah. So in this book there is a blending of streams of thinking and writing which had previously been diverse.

After the translator's preface, chapters 1 to 42:14 consist of a collection of wisdom sayings arranged in groups according to topics. Next follows a section praising the mighty deeds of God, first in creation (42:15–43:33), then in history (chapters 44–50). Ben Sirach reviews the whole history of Israel, and its pre-history as well. He dwells in turn on each of the great figures of the past, and refers the glory to the Lord who, through the persons and events of history, has "displayed his greatness from earliest times" (44:2). In chapter 51 are two poems which sum up the life of the author.

As in other books, Wisdom is personified in Ecclesiasticus. Chapter 24 contains a beautiful poem in which Wisdom speaks of herself, her origins with God, and her coming to live in Israel. Finally, Wisdom compares herself to the tree of life, and the author, identifying her with the torah, compares her to the rivers of paradise.

The Wisdom of God

Jesus came as a teacher of wisdom. His sayings and teachings are in line with the whole wisdom tradition of Israel, both in terms of what he had to say and of how he said it. He taught how to live well, in a way that is pleasing to God. He took special care with "the little ones." He spoke in parables, proverbs and riddles, and gave special instruction to his pupils on the meaning of his sayings (compare Prov 1:2–6).

For his disciples, of course, Jesus was *the* Teacher of wisdom, and indeed Wisdom in person.

Eventually, John the evangelist, reflecting both on the mystery of Jesus and on the biblical portrayal of divine Wisdom as a person (e.g., Prov 8:22–31), was able to start his Gospel: "In the beginning was the Word: the Word was with God and the Word was God. Through him all things came to be; not one thing had its being but through him. . . . The Word was made flesh, he lived among us, and we saw his glory, the glory that is his as the only Son of the Father, full of grace and truth" (Jn 1:1–3, 14).

Jesus is therefore in the fullest sense the Wisdom of God. St. Paul, however, reminds us that God's Wisdom appears to be foolishness when judged by human standards. For it is a Wisdom that is revealed upon the cross (see 1 Cor 1:17ff). The Wisdom that is Jesus is a paradox and a puzzle.

For Study or Discussion

1. "The fear of the Lord is the beginning of wisdom." What does this mean?

2. How do the wisdom books teach us to live well?

3. What light do the wisdom books throw on the problem of suffering?

4. "God wants to give all people knowledge of himself." What light do the wisdom books throw on this?

5. How do the wisdom books look forward to the coming of Christ?

6. "The Song of Songs can be read as the pivotal book of the Bible." What do you think of this?

12

Messengers of God

The Books of the Prophets ◊ What Is a Prophet? ◊ The Prophets: Samuel, Elijah and Elisha ◊ Isaiah ◊ Jeremiah, Lamentations, Baruch ◊ Ezekiel ◊ Daniel ◊ The Twelve ◊ Apocalyptic ◊ The Message of the Prophets: (1) The One God ◊ (2) The Holy God ◊ (3) The Messiah ◊ The Messenger Who Was the Message

The Books of the Prophets

The great commentators on the events of Israel's history are the prophets. The historical books which we considered in Chapters Five and Six—Joshua, Judges, Samuel, Kings—reflect their views on the events narrated, so that the Jews call these books "the former prophets."

The Book of Deuteronomy, the final restatement of the law of the covenant, also reflects the outlook of the prophets. In it are to be found clearly stated the "issues" of Israel's history: if the people kept the covenant God had made with them they would enjoy his blessings, and, in particular, they would enjoy possession of the land he had given them. Otherwise they would not (see Deut 29–30).

The prophetical books of the Catholic Bible are the four major prophets—Isaiah, Jeremiah (with Lamentations and Baruch), Ezekiel and Daniel—and the twelve minor prophets—Hosea, Joel, Amos, Obadiah, Jonah, Micah, Nahum, Habakkuk, Zephaniah, Haggai, Zechariah and Malachi. (In the Douay Bible, many of these names are spelled differently.)

What Is a Prophet?

We think of a prophet as one who foretells the future. Foretelling the future was, however, only one of the things the Hebrew prophets did. They were men and women who spoke out. More specifically they spoke out on behalf of God.

The first of the prophets was really Moses, with whom God used to speak "face to face, as a man speaks with his friend" (Ex 33:11). Moses had spoken to the people on behalf of God at the time of the exodus, the making of the covenant, and the giving of the law. God promised him that after the people had entered the promised land, he would raise up for them, from among their own, "a prophet like yourself. . . . I will put my words into his mouth, and he shall tell them all I command him" (Deut 18:18).

A prophet was, therefore, a person called and inspired by God to deliver a message on his behalf. The message might be for an individual, for Israel as a whole, or even for the Gentile nations. The Bible often states: "The word of the Lord came to . . . " The prophets themselves would begin their message by saying: "Hear the word of the Lord."

It was the task of the prophets to tell people how God saw things, in the present or the future, or even in the past. (The historical books are the story of Israel's past seen through the eyes of God.) Besides words, the prophets used a variety of symbols, including mime, to deliver their message. Even their words consisted largely of imagery, often making very beautiful poetry.

Other Eastern nations and religions besides Israel had "prophets." But the Hebrew prophets were true prophets, because they spoke on behalf of the true God. They confirmed their message from the Lord by foretelling future events which actually came to pass, such as the destruction of the invading Assyrian army (Isaiah 36–37) or the fall of Jerusalem to the Babylonians (Jer 9).

These events had been brought about by the God who spoke of them beforehand through his prophets. By contrast, what the false prophets foretold did not take place, and the false gods were powerless to foresee, let alone to influence, future events.

The Prophets : Samuel, Elijah and Elisha

Prophecy in Israel dates from earliest times. The great Samuel (after 1040 B.C.) is regarded not only as a judge and a priest, but also as a "seer," i.e., as a prophet (1 Sam 9:9). Other "seers" existed in those days as well.

There were in fact many prophets in Israel. Often they formed communities or schools ("the sons of the prophets"). Some prophets, however, stood out from the rest, and their ministries are recorded in the Bible. In any given case this written record ("the Book of the Prophet") may have been composed not by the prophet himself but by a disciple or by other members of his community. Several of the prophetical books are actually compilations of material originating in different periods but regarded nevertheless as associated in some way with the prophet of the title.

The great age of the prophets was the period of the monarchy. The prophets Nathan and Gad brought the word of God to David. After the division, the northern kingdom produced those mighty men of God Elijah and Elisha (around 850 B.C.) whose deeds are recorded in the Books of Kings. By their preaching and their actions they tried to bring back the people and their rulers to the pure worship of the true God and to the practice of justice according to the covenant.

Elijah suffered persecution but was rewarded with a revelation of God on his holy mountain (1 Kgs 19). He thus resembled Moses (compare Ex 33:18–34:9), and so Moses and Elijah sum up the Old Testament ("the law and the prophets").

Isaiah

The southern kingdom was the scene of the ministry of Isaiah (from 740 B.C.) during the period when the Assyrians invaded the country, conquered the northern capital Samaria, and threatened Jerusalem. The first part of the Book of Isaiah, chapters 1–39, contains his preaching (as well as some historical episodes).

It is one of the high points of the Bible, both from the grandeur of its contents and from the beauty of its poetical style.

Isaiah was concerned with the majesty and holiness of the God whom he had seen in a vision and who had sent him to preach to his own people (Is 6). His preaching consisted both of threats and promises. He foretold the downfall of hostile neighbors, but in the name of God he denounced his own nation too. Its ritual observances cloaked moral faults and social injustice. Its trust was not in God alone but in politics and diplomacy. All these sins and failings would be punished. Yet God would not let his people be utterly destroyed by their enemies.

The remaining sections of the Book of Isaiah, from chapter 40 onward—and also some earlier passages—date from a later period than the ministry of Isaiah himself but have always been included in the book which bears his name and no doubt stem from "the school of Isaiah." The second part consists of chapters 40–55. It dates from the period at the end of the exile in Babylon (around 550 B.C.) and is probably by a single author (sometimes called "Deutero-Isaiah," i.e., "Second Isaiah"). He foretells the return to Jerusalem, which will eventually become the religious center of the world as the pagan nations are converted to recognize and worship the only true God.

Included in the second part of the Book of Isaiah are four poems known as the Songs of the Servant of Yahweh (42:1–9; 49:1–6; 50:4–11; 52:13–53:12). Elsewhere in the book, the nation of Israel is addressed as the Lord's servant. In these songs, however, the "servant" seems to be an individual who represents the nation and yet at the same time has his own personal identity and destiny. The servant is called to bring back Israel and also to be the light of the nations, so that God's salvation may reach to the ends of the earth. This vocation will entail apparent failure and bitter suffering. Yet it is the sins of others he bears as well as the punishment due to them, and in the end God will champion his cause.

The third part of the Book of Isaiah consists of chapters 56 to 66 and seems to be a collection of pieces from more than one author. The themes of many of these pieces are closely related to those of "Deutero-Isaiah." However, they probably date from a somewhat later period, after the exile.

Taken altogether, the Book of Isaiah is one of the most sheerly beautiful and heartwarming books of the Bible. The second part has been described as "the Book of Consolation." But on practically every page of the entire work, God assures us of his undying love for us. "Does a woman forget her baby at the breast, or fail to cherish the son of her womb? Yet even if these forget, I will never forget you" (49:15).

Jeremiah, Lamentations, Baruch

During the crisis which led to the fall of Jerusalem and the Babylonian captivity, the word of God was delivered to the kings and people of Judah by Jeremiah (from 627 B.C.). He too has left a book which is one of the masterpieces of the Bible. It was Jeremiah's bitter duty to try to awaken his fellow countrymen from their false sense of security and to show them the imminent catastrophe to which they were shutting their eyes. His vocation to be God's messenger entailed great sufferings (see, for instance, chapters 18 and 20).

Jeremiah stands close in thought and style to the Book of Deuteronomy. He sees the covenant as a pact of love between God and his people. The people have broken the covenant and rejected God's love (see, for instance, chapter 2). For this reason God has allowed them to be punished by the Babylonians. But he has not disowned them entirely. Chastened by their sufferings, they will turn back to God, who will make a new covenant with them (31:31–34). Their exile will come to an end when God strikes down their oppressors and brings them back to the land he gave them.

Immediately following the Book of Jeremiah and traditionally (but probably wrongly) attributed to him is the Book of Lamentations. This is a series of poems mourning the destruction of Jerusalem by the Babylonians in 587 B.C. In language of stark and poignant beauty the Book of Lamentations conveys the shock and grief of those who looked on the ruins of their sacred and beloved city and saw its men, women and children slaughtered, dying of hunger and disease, or led into captivity.

These poems register human emotions at various levels. On one level they speak for all who have experienced such horrors, as does another ancient masterpiece, "The Women of Troy" by the Greek Euripides. They are sung by the Jews every year on the commemoration of the destruction of the temple and thus give voice to the affliction of so many centuries of exile and persecution. In the Christian liturgy they were until recently sung during Holy Week to express the Church's desolation at the death of its Lord.

The Book of Jeremiah was compiled with the assistance of the prophet's secretary Baruch. A short book goes under his name. It appears, however, to date from a later period and to reflect the situation of the Jews in the diaspora. Its themes are repentance, wisdom, and the foolishness of idolatry.

Ezekiel

Ezekiel (from about 600 B.C.) was the great prophet of the exile. A deportee himself, he lived through the time just before and after the final siege of Jerusalem. He was called to sustain the hope of Israel in a future resurrection of the nation. God will bring back Israel for the sake of his own holy name (see chapters 36 and 37).

Ezekiel is close in spirit to those whose great concern was with the law and with the worship of God. It was in these circles, consisting mainly of priests, that most of the legal and liturgical material of the first five books of the Bible was preserved and developed. Not that these people were interested only or even mainly in rules. They were imbued with a deep sense of the holiness of God, which is reflected in the opening vision of the Book of Ezekiel. The prophet looks forward to a future in which Israel, purified by God of all her sins, will become a holy nation (see chapters 40–48).

Daniel

The Book of Daniel is not counted by the Jews as one of the prophetical books, and in fact, although it is set in the period of the exile in Babylon, it seems to date from a much later period. It was probably written by a Jew living during the Maccabean revolt (about 167 B.C.). The author wanted to encourage his fellow Jews not to give way under pagan pressure but to remain faithful to their own religion. In composing his book which he wrote in the Aramaic language, he made use of material which did come down from the time of the exile and dealt with a Jewish deportee named Daniel. He seems to have been a man about whom many stories were told—two which are not in the Hebrew Bible have come down in the ancient Greek translation known as the Septuagint: Bel and the Dragon, and the Trial of Susanna.

The Book of Daniel as we have it is in two parts. The first part, chapters 1–6, tells how Daniel and his three friends are brought up at the royal court of Babylon and acquire power and influence, yet are faithful to their religion. The three friends refuse to obey instructions to adore the king's statue but are miraculously saved from the "burning fiery furnace." Daniel meanwhile interprets the dreams of King Nebuchadnezzar and the vision of the handwriting on the wall at Belshazzar's feast which predicts the conquest of the Babylonian empire by the Medes and Persians. He himself disobeys the orders of the King to worship him and is thrown into the lions' den but escapes unharmed.

The second part, chapters 7–12, consists of dreams and visions of Daniel. All of them have reference to the situation of the Jewish people at the time the book was written. One of these visions (in chapter 7) features four beasts which, like the four metals of the statue in the dream of King Nebuchadnezzar, represent four ancient empires: the Babylonians, the Medes, the Persians, and the Greeks. In the same vision, Daniel sees "coming on the clouds of heaven one like a son of man" (7:13). The term "son of man" had already been used by Ezekiel to mean simply "man." Here, like the servant of Yahweh, the son of man is a mysterious figure who is identified with a group ("the saints of the Most High") and at the same time is an individual who in his own person undergoes suffering at the hands of the powers of evil but is finally upheld by God.

The Twelve

The twelve "minor prophets"—so called because the books they have left are shorter, not necessarily because they themselves are of lesser importance—are considered as a single book in the Hebrew Bible ("The Twelve"). In fact they represent the whole range of themes that are to be found in the "major prophets," and among their writings are some of the gems of the Bible.

The twelve cover a timescale of about three hundred years. The earliest, and in fact the first prophet whose teachings have come down to us in a separate book, was Amos who lived in the northern kingdom about 750 B.C. A little later, also in the north, came Hosea. Micah was a contemporary of Isaiah in the southern kingdom about 735. A century later, about 630, Zephaniah appeared about the same time as Jeremiah. Nahum and Habakkuk both flourished before 600. The ministry of Haggai and Zechariah coincided with the rebuilding of Jerusalem and the founding of the second temple (about 520 B.C.). Malachi and Obadiah date from the period 450–400, and Joel about 350. A little later, the Book of Jonah was written (see Chapter Eight of this book).

Apocalyptic

Among the prophetical books are passages which belong to a class of writing called "apocalyptic," from the Greek word "apocalypse" which means "revelation." These writings lift the veil which hides the future and give a glimpse of things that are yet to come.

The revelation is often conveyed in visions, which may feature angels or other supernatural beings, or even monstrous animals like the beasts of heraldry and mythology. These and other details of the visions are obviously symbolic. Their meaning was presumably clearer to contemporaries than it sometimes is to us, and in fact one often has the impression of being in the presence of a coded message.

The apocalyptic strain is strong in Ezekiel and even stronger in Daniel, but it is found in other prophetic writings as well, including Zechariah, Joel and the third part of Isaiah. It is also found outside the prophetical books. The Book of Judith could be considered an apocalypse. The New Testament contains apocalyptic: a whole book called the Apocalypse or Revelation of John, and also important sections of the Gospels (Mt 24–25; Mk 13; Lk 21). It is also a form frequently employed to describe certain ancient writings which have not found their way into the Bible (such as the Books of Esdras and Enoch and the Testaments of the Twelve Patriarchs).

The future which is uncovered in apocalyptic is the climax toward which the events of the here and now are already tending. It is therefore the key to the meaning of the present. The climax is a crisis—literally a judgment—in which good and evil are pitted against one another in a final struggle. After seeming to get the upper hand, the forces of evil, enemies of Israel and of God, will be defeated by the direct intervention of God himself.

This divine intervention will be the "day of the Lord" foretold by many of the prophets, beginning with Amos. It will be a time of testing for Israel, but ultimately of deliverance, at least for "the true Israel," those who are faithful to God, his "saints." The drama will involve the whole human race and will have the entire universe as its theater.

Such an outcome involves the passing away of the world as we know it, even the end of the present created universe. Many of the apocalyptic writings are marked by imagery of the unmaking of the cosmos (the reversal, therefore, of the creation imagery of Genesis): sun and moon darkened, stars falling from heaven, the seas breaking their bounds. However, the end is not the return of primeval chaos. There will be a new heaven and a new earth which will be at the same time the renewal of the original creation which was spoiled by human sin.

Meanwhile, now that the issue has been made clear, we have to take sides. Now is the time of decision. Hence the great sense of urgency which pervades these writings.

The Message of the Prophets: (1) The One God

The message of the prophets—that is, God's message delivered by them—had three main points. The first was: there is only one God. The prophets resisted all attempts to combine the worship of the true God with the worship of other gods. This was a temptation to which kings and and people were constantly giving way.

Yahweh is the only God of Israel. The prophets insistently presented the demands of the jealous love of God for his people. Several of them, especially Hosea, made use of the love of husband and wife to illustrate the love which God had for Israel. Israel was an unfaithful wife, but God still loved her.

Yahweh is the only true God. The prophets all speak of God as Maker and Master of the whole world and of everything in it. He is the Lord of all nations and the Governor of their destinies. Compared with him, the other so-called "gods" are nothing. In fact they do not even really exist.

(2) The Holy God

The prophets taught that sin is an offense against God. Sacrifices by themselves were not enough. The people had to keep the holy law of the holy God, to be holy because God is holy, to be set apart for the God who is himself apart, especially separated from sin.

The law of the covenant included justice between individuals and in society itself. From Elijah onward, the prophets repeated that injustice to one's neighbor broke the covenant just as much as did idolatry (in fact the two often went together). Amos was the great prophet of social justice and in the name of God denounced the oppression of the poor by the rich.

The requirements of the holy God were thus summed up by Micah (6:8)—"to act justly, to love tenderly, and to walk humbly with your God."

(3) The Messiah

The prophets also foretold that God would send his Anointed One, his Messiah or Christ (Hebrew and Greek words respectively meaning "anointed"). They often had to threaten the people with disaster in the name of God. But they were also the messengers of his promises of consolation. A remnant of the erring nation would be left, and among this remnant God would establish his own kingdom. The ruler of this kingdom would be anointed by God, and so would be known as the Messiah or Christ.

Kings were anointed as part of their investiture, and in the Bible "the Lord's anointed" usually means the king. Hence the Messiah would be a king, a descendant of David. However, as hopes placed in earthly kings were disappointed, the Messiah was seen more and more as a heavenly figure and merged with other mysterious personages, such as the servant of Yahweh and the son of man. His coming was ardently awaited by those who "looked forward to Israel's comforting" (Lk 2:25).

The Messenger Who Was the Message

God's promise to raise up a prophet like Moses was fulfilled in part every time a prophet arose in Israel. It was finally fulfilled in Jesus, whose hearers recognized him as "a great prophet" (Lk 7:16) and even as "the one Moses wrote about in the law, the one about whom the prophets wrote" (Jn 1:45).

Jesus was a prophet, a messenger from God, or rather *the* Prophet, *the* Messenger. For whereas "at various times in the past and in various ways, God spoke to our ancestors through the prophets . . . in our own time, the last days, he has spoken to us through his Son" (Heb 1:1–2).

But Jesus was even more than that. God had promised that when he raised up a prophet like Moses, he would put his own words into his mouth (Deut 18:18). Jesus was not only the mouthpiece of God, but himself God's Word (Jn 1:1–2, 14). He was the Message of God as well as the Messenger. God spoke to us not only through Jesus but in Jesus.

For Study or Discussion

1. "The prophets had to tell the people how God sees things." What did this entail?

2. Was the prophet's vocation an easy one?

3. What does God tell us about himself through the prophets?

4. Christians are meant to be "prophets." What does this mean? What can we learn from the Old Testament prophets?

5. How did the prophets prepare the way for the coming of Christ?

6. Was Jesus a prophet?

13

The New Testament

A New Testament ◊ A New Covenant ◊ Fulfilling the Law and the Prophets ◊ The Old Testament in the New

A New Testament

To the first generations of Christians "the Scriptures" meant the Jewish Scriptures, that is, what we know as the Old Testament. Gradually, however, they produced a literature of their own, some of which came to be recognized by the Church as having the same status as the Jewish holy books, and so to be Scripture.

The Christian Scriptures, known as the New Testament, consist of twenty-seven "books." The core of the Christian Scriptures, occupying a position somewhat like that of the torah or Pentateuch in the Jewish Scriptures, are the four Gospels of Matthew, Mark, Luke and John. Then comes the Acts of the Apostles. There follow a series of letters, of which thirteen bear the name of St. Paul, while a fourteenth, addressed to "the Hebrews," has traditionally been associated with Paul, and the remaining seven bear the names of James, Peter, John, and Jude. The final book of the New Testament is the Apocalypse or Revelation of St. John.

Calling these writings a "New Testament" implies a very definite view of their nature and of their relationship to the rest of the Bible. For these Christian Scriptures are not simply added on to the already existing Scriptures. At the time when most of them were being written, the Jewish canon, or official list, of Scripture was still open. Yet these books, composed for the most part by

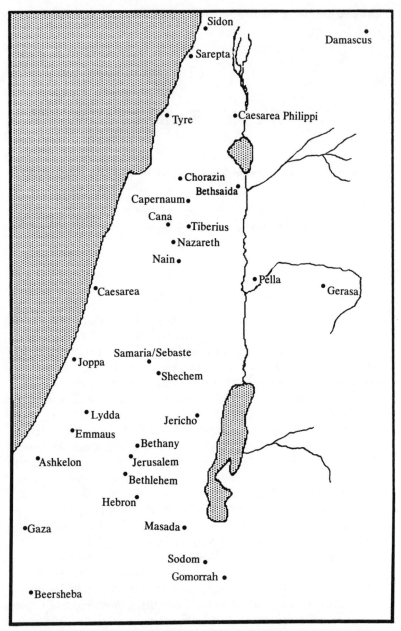

THE HOLY LAND IN THE NEW TESTAMENT PERIOD

Jews, were not simply included among the miscellaneous group of "writings" which formed the third part of the Jewish Bible. Nor did these Christian books settle for the status of commentaries or reflections upon the Scriptures, like the mass of writings produced by both Jews and Christians during the following centuries. On the other hand, the Christian Scriptures did not supersede the Jewish Scriptures.

Instead of all these possibilities, the Christian Church saw them as "the New Testament," face to face with "the Old Testament" and together forming the whole body of Scripture, or the Bible. There was continuity with what had gone before, and the Jewish heritage retained its value. But something new had happened, and the Jewish Scriptures had been fulfilled.

A New Covenant

The new thing which the Christians claimed had taken place was that God had made a new, and this time everlasting, covenant with the human race. We have seen that the theme of "covenant" runs right through the Bible, starting with Abraham (or before, with Noah or even Adam), through Moses at Mount Sinai, to David and beyond. The prophets had continually returned to the solemn agreement between the Lord and Israel, by which he became their God and they became his people.

At the same time, the prophets frequently had to denounce Israel's unfaithfulness to the covenant, and even to declare that they had rendered it null and void (see Ez 16:59). At such times, they foreshadowed the making of a new covenant, which would not be broken as the previous one was, and which would be written on the hearts of the people (see Jer 31:31–34).

The Christians declared that this new covenant had in fact been made (see Heb 8:6–7). It was announced by Jesus Christ, signed and sealed in the blood which he shed on the cross, and ratified by his resurrection. God had thereby established a new relationship, not just with Israel, but with the whole of humanity. To enter into this relationship oneself, one had to believe in Jesus as Messiah and Lord.

This new covenant or relationship between God and human

beings is the theme of the Christian Scriptures, which reflect its various aspects. It was for this reason that the collection of books which make up the Christian Scriptures came to be called "the new covenant" or more usually (for the two words mean more or less the same thing) "the New Testament." At the same time, the Jewish Scriptures, which had the previous covenant or covenants for a theme, became known to the Christians as "the Old Testament."

Fulfilling the Law and the Prophets

As already mentioned, the Old Testament is not superseded or rendered obsolete by the New (despite the possible connotations of the words "old" and "new"). The Old Testament is, however, interpreted by the New. More precisely, it is interpreted by Christ and finds its definitive meaning in him. Jesus himself said that he had not come to abolish the law or the prophets (in other words, the Scriptures) but to fulfill them (Mt 5:17). He came to be the completion or fulfillment which the Jewish Scriptures themselves looked ahead to and prepared for.

Jesus fulfilled the law, that is, the torah or Pentateuch. This was both the story of God's choice of Israel and also the record of the covenant he made with his people and the law he gave them. The story was told and retold many times over, in the successive versions of the Pentateuch as it took shape, and in the later books of the Bible. Such retelling not only kept alive the memory of the original events. It also reminded the people that the God who had acted in this way for them in the past would do so again. Later events in the history of Israel, such as the return from the exile, were seen as fulfilling this promise. Remembering past deliverance awoke the unquenchable hope of a future and final liberation, an irrevocable choice, an unbreakable union between God and his people. It was this hope that Jesus came to fulfill.

Jesus also fulfilled the torah as covenant and law. We have already seen that the prophets had foretold a new covenant which would complete the old. The law of Moses itself was not complete. It held in check human passions and tendencies which otherwise would have been destructive. Thus it forbade murder and adultery; it gave some protection to a divorced wife; it forbade oath-breaking; it put limits on the taking of revenge; it commanded love of one's fellow Israelite. This was already a great deal, but it fell short of the perfection of human behavior. The new law of Jesus forbade anger and interior lust, divorce and the taking of oaths, retaliation or even resistance, and it commanded the love of one's enemies (see Mt 5:20–48).

The completion or fulfillment of the law was the guiding theme of much of Jesus' teaching. In all the instances just mentioned, Jesus went to the heart of the commandment in the law of Moses, found its thrust and followed that through to the completion which the previous commandment fell short of but which it prepared for. So the commandment "You must not kill" did not deal with the anger which is at the origin of many crimes of violence; Jesus' commandment outlaws anger against one's brother. To love one's fellow Israelite still left the rest of the human race outside the bounds of one's love; to love one's enemies, that is, all "outsiders," breaks down the barriers and gives love its complete scope. Finally, all the commandments can be summed up in the one: "Love your neighbor as yourself," so love is the ultimate fulfillment of the law (see Mt 22:34–40; Rom 13:8–10).

Jesus also fulfilled the prophets. At the beginning of his public ministry, Luke tells us (4:16–22), Jesus went into the synagogue at Nazareth on the sabbath, read from the Scriptures and preached on the reading. The passage he read was from Isaiah 61:1–2: "The Spirit of the Lord is upon me; therefore he has anointed me. He has sent me to bring glad tidings to the poor, to proclaim liberty to captives, recovery of sight to the blind and release to prisoners, to announce a year of favor from the Lord." Jesus' message to his hearers was: "Today this Scripture passage is fulfilled in your hearing."

This seems to have been characteristic of Jesus' own use of the Bible. He would point out that the God who had acted in the past or who had made a promise in the past—as the Scriptures said he had—was acting now, in this way, in these events, persons, and circumstances. So the Scriptures and "today" throw light on one another and give meaning to one another. The Bible shows the sort of thing God did and said in the past, and so gives the clue to discover what he is doing or saying *now*. By the same token, what God is seen to be doing now, fulfills the Scripture and gives meaning to it today. Once we know how to read the Scriptures, we can read "the signs of the times" (see Mt 16:3). But unless we can read the signs of the times, we will not find the true meaning of the Scriptures.

The meaning that Jesus saw both in the Scriptures and in the signs of the times was that his hearers stood before a turning point, a moment of truth—or, rather, before *the* turning point, *the* moment of truth, the crisis, in every sense of the word. The "last times" were upon them. God was establishing his kingdom. And Jesus himself was sent by God not only to proclaim the coming of the kingdom, but actually to bring it into the world. God was dealing finally and decisively with the human race through and in Jesus. The Scriptures were being fulfilled by Jesus even as his hearers listened. It was the time of testing and the hour of judgment. It was world's ending and new creation.

The Old Testament in the New

In Luke's Gospel (24: 44–48), the risen Jesus points out to his disciples all that was written about himself "in the law of Moses and in the prophets and in the psalms"—in other words, in the whole of the Jewish Scriptures. The New Testament in fact reflects a highly developed system of interpreting the Scriptures, i.e., the Old Testament, in terms of Christ. It was at the same time a system of interpreting Christ—the true significance of who he was and what he did—in terms of the Old Testament. This system of interpretation was continued by Christian writers for many centuries and was summed up in the saying: "The New Testament lies hidden in the Old, and the Old Testament is made plain in the New."

The first Christians claimed that they knew the real meaning of Jesus of Nazareth and the real meaning of the Scriptures. The two were very closely linked. The real meaning of Jesus was to be found in the Scriptures, and the real meaning of the Scriptures was to be found in Jesus. Those who rejected the Church's interpretation of Jesus rejected also its interpretation of the Scriptures.

On the other hand, to understand what the New Testament says about Jesus, it was—and is—necessary to know something about the Old Testament.

The first Christians, enlightened by the Holy Spirit, were able to see the chief persons, events and institutions of the Old Testament, and in particular of "the law of Moses" (the Pentateuch), as foreshadowing Christ. It was as if he—"the One to come"—had cast his shadow before him, a shadow which was already visible in Israel. So, for instance, Paul in Romans 5:14 says that Adam "prefigured" Christ, and the Letter to the Hebrews portrays the Christian life as an exodus and a journey toward the promised land (chapters 3–4:11), and the whole system of sacrifice and priesthood in the Pentateuch as fulfilled by the sacrifice and priesthood of Christ (chapters 4:14–10:18). Readers will already have encountered these and similar examples of early Christian interpretation of the Old Testament in terms of Christ in previous chapters of this book.

For his disciples looking back on the events of his life, death and resurrection, Jesus was the Prophet foretold by God to Moses in Deuteronomy 18:18 (see the sermon of Peter at Pentecost in Acts 3:20–24). He was also the one about whom "all the prophets" had spoken. In the Gospels, the whole life of Jesus is seen as the fulfillment of prophecy: the circumstances of his birth, his ministry of teaching and healing, his rejection, suffering, death, and resurrection. It was above all in his passion that Jesus fulfilled not only particular prophecies, but the whole notion of the prophet's vocation, as that was seen in the light of the life of Jeremiah and of the whole line of prophets whose blood was shed by those to whom they were sent (see Mt 23:30). In particular, Jesus fulfilled the prophecy of the suffering servant in Isaiah 52:13–53:12. This passage is often echoed in the New Testament and seems to have been used as a basic text in the early Church's work of evangelization. In Acts 8:34–35, we learn that the Ethiopian eunuch reading these words asked the deacon Philip whether the prophet spoke them of himself or of someone else, and that Philip, starting from this text of Scripture, announced to him the good news of Jesus.

As for "the psalms," there are in fact about one hundred and twenty quotations from the psalms in the New Testament, one-third of the total number of Old Testament quotations. This frequency of quotation no doubt reflects the familiarity of both writers and readers with the psalms, which were used by the Jews in their daily prayers. It also reflects the whole process, already mentioned in Chapter Ten, whereby the Jews had come to regard King David not only as the author of the psalms but as a prophet. The psalms already pointed ahead to the Messiah. Now their predictions were seen to have been fulfilled in Jesus the Christ. The psalmist had foreseen details of the passion (see Jn 19:24 with Ps 22:18, and Jn 19:36 with Ps 34:20). In the Acts of the Apostles, the first Christians frequently quote the psalms as foretelling the events they were witnessing: thus 1:20, quoting Psalms 69:25 and 109:8, on the replacement of Judas; 2:25–28, quoting Psalm 16:8–11, on the resurrection of Jesus; 2:35, quoting Psalm 110:1, on Jesus as the Messiah.

It was above all Psalms 2 and 110, messianic psalms par excellence, which were applied to Christ and found to be fulfilled in him, as many quotations and references in the New Testament show. Jesus himself had drawn attention to the unsolved riddle of Psalm 110 when he asked how, if the Messiah was the son of David, David himself could call him "Lord" (Mk 12:35–37). After the resurrection of Jesus, his disciples had the answer.

For Study or Discussion

1. Is the Old Testament relevant for Christians?

2. How did Jesus fulfill the law?

3. How did Jesus fulfill the prophets?

14

The World of the New Testament

In the Roman Empire ◊ Judaism in the New Testament Period: Pharisees, Sadducees, Herodians, Zealots, Essenes

In the Roman Empire

The world in which the events of the New Testament took place—both the life of Christ and the early spread of Christianity—was part of the Roman empire. The Romans did not, however, exercise their control everywhere in the same way.

At the time of Jesus' birth, Judea, Samaria, Galilee, the Golan and neighboring districts in the north, and Perea on the east bank of the Jordan formed the kingdom of Herod the Great, under Roman "protection." To the south and east of the Sea of Galilee was a confederation of about ten city states known as the Decapolis, which was also in the Roman orbit. At Herod's death his kingdom was divided: Archelaus took Judea and Samaria, Antipas took Galilee and Perea, and Philip took the remaining territories in the north. Eventually, the Romans deposed Archelaus and established direct rule in Judea and Samaria under a series of governors, of whom Pontius Pilate was one. Herod Antipas and Philip retained their principalities with the title of "tetrarch." They are both mentioned in the Gospels. On two occasions after the time of Christ but within the period described by the Acts of the Apostles, the Romans partially restored Herod the Great's kingdom in favor of two of his descendants, Agrippa I and Agrippa II.

Further afield, in Syria, Asia Minor and Greece, all visited by St. Paul on his missionary journeys, the normal political unit was the city or city state, which was a legacy of the great wave of Greek expansion in earlier centuries, when new cities were founded, or existing towns re-formed, on the model of the ancient Greek city states. These enjoyed a large measure of internal self-government and administered their own laws among their own citizens. Over the cities in each province was the Roman governor. He commanded the Roman army in those provinces which were garrisoned and administered justice where Roman law or Roman citizens were concerned. Roman citizenship was a privilege extended to certain individuals or to citizens of specially favored cities within the empire. Paul was a Roman citizen. Jesus was not.

Taxes and customs dues had to be paid to the Roman state, as well as to various local governments. At this time, the Roman government used to let out the right to gather taxes due to itself to private individuals by tender. The tax farmer, known as a "publican," contracted to provide the required sum. It was understood that the expenses of the enterprise and his own profit came out of the pockets of the taxpayers. The system obviously lent itself to corruption and extortion, and the publicans and their local agents were consequently feared and hated. Among Jews there was also the added infamy that they were collaborators with the regime. The tax collectors of the Gospels were very much on the fringes of respectable society, even beyond the pale, and were classed with other "sinners."

Throughout the eastern Mediterranean, Greek was the "lingua franca." This reflected its position as the language both of commerce and of "higher culture." With a knowledge of Greek one could move anywhere. Similarly, books written in Greek could be read immediately in Athens, Ephesus, Antioch, Alexandria and Rome. The various books which make up the New Testament, at least by the time they had reached a final form and were ready for widespread circulation, were written in Greek. Most Christians read the Old Testament in a translation from the Greek.

Judaism in the New Testament Period

The Judaism of the time of Christ presented a very varied picture. There were, in fact, within it a number of different movements or parties (of which, for a long time, Christianity seemed to be one). The New Testament itself mentions several of these: Pharisees, Sadducees, Herodians, and Zealots. Another group, the Essenes, are not mentioned in the New Testament but are mentioned by contemporaries, and are now well known to us through their own writings. We will look briefly at each of these in turn.

The *Pharisees* (whose name means "separated") descended from the observant Jews of the Maccabean period and, ultimately, from the movement of reform begun by Ezra after the exile. They were only a minority within the whole body of Judaism, but they had an influence far beyond their numbers, especially with the common people. They owed their influence not only to their religious devotion, but also to the fact that they showed concern for the religious life of ordinary people and for their ability to keep the law. This latter trait was especially characteristic of the school of Hillel, which opposed the stricter views of the school of Shammai.

The covenant and the law were the chief concerns of the Pharisees. The Babylonian exile and other national misfortunes were, they believed, due to failure to keep faith with God. On the other hand, perfect observance of the law by Israel would bring in the age of the Messiah. The scribes of the Pharisee party dedicated themselves to set out clearly what the law was in every circumstance of life, and also to "build a hedge" about the law, so that it would not be broken by ignorance or carelessness. Thus, as well as the "written torah" there came to be also an "unwritten torah" which was regarded as descending, through the "traditions of the elders," from Moses himself. The full development of the "unwritten torah" came only after the time of Christ, but it was already a characteristic feature of Pharisaic Judaism.

The heart of the religion of the Pharisees was the covenant-relationship of the nation and of the individual with God. This relationship was based on the free choice of God and it implied corresponding obligations, both of worship and of moral behavior. It could be broken by sin and restored, through the mercy of God, by repentance.

The Pharisees, therefore, represented a great deal of what was best in Jewish religion. They certainly do not deserve to be thought of simply as hypocrites and hair-splitting legalists. It is no coincidence that the golden rule—to do to others as you would have them do to you—is attributed both to Jesus (Mt 7:12) and, in a somewhat different form, to the Pharisee Rabbi Hillel. (It is also in the Book of Tobit 4:15.) Both Jesus and Hillel declare it to represent the essence of the torah. Indeed, despite his vigorous criticisms of the Pharisees, Jesus stands closer to them than to any other party in contemporary Judaism. In any case, his arguments with them (which, as they are reported to us in the Gospels, may well be colored by later conflicts) are arguments "within the family," and the Pharisees argued with one another no less forcefully. It was still Jew versus Jew. The same expressions bear a very different character when they are turned against the Jewish people and their religion by non-Jews.

In politics, the Pharisees were patriots but realists too. They were not collaborators with the Roman occupying power, but on the other hand they were opposed to any attempt to oust the Romans by force. Most of them were against the revolt of A.D. 66. The result was that, in the general ruin of Palestinian Judaism which followed the catastrophe of A.D. 70, the Pharisee party alone remained relatively intact, and one of their leaders, Rabbi Yohanan ben Zakkai, was permitted by Emperor Vespasian to establish a rabbinical school at Yavneh (Jamnia). This school became the focus of the reconstruction of Judaism in the years which followed the fall of Jerusalem, and eventually the way of the Pharisees became the dominant form of Judaism. It was a Judaism now without kingship or temple, but centered single-mindedly on torah and on the attempt to build a personal and social life based on it.

Although many Pharisees, including St. Paul, came to believe in Jesus as the Messiah, the Pharisee party as such did not accept the Gospel. The years following the fall of Jerusalem saw the eventual exclusion of the Christians from the body of Judaism.

There were now two new religions issuing from ancient Israel and the Judaism of the second temple, each claiming to be the true heir and interpreter of the tradition.

The *Sadducees* (whose name is obscure) came from the well-to-do and aristocratic classes and most of them belonged to priestly families (though not all priests were Sadducees). Their central concerns were the temple and its liturgy. They seem to have been rigorists in their interpretation of the law. They were also highly conservative: they accepted only the "written torah" of the Pentateuch, and not the "unwritten torah" of the Pharisees, and they also rejected certain doctrines which had developed more recently in Judaism and were held by the Pharisees—the soul and its afterlife with rewards and punishments, resurrection, angels and demons. They were not popular, and their influence and even their existence depended on the temple. When it disappeared, so did they.

The *Herodians* appear to have been a party of politically-minded Jews who were supporters of the royal family.

The *Zealots* were also politically minded, but in a different direction. They were violently opposed to Roman rule in the holy land and, inspired by the revolt of Mattathias and the Maccabees, continually rose in armed rebellion. The Zealots were among the leading spirits in the war of 66–70, and a number of them held out at Massada until May 74, when they committed suicide rather than surrender. The Zealot movement seems to have had its base in Galilee, and one of the twelve chosen by Jesus, Simon, was nicknamed "the Zealot," possibly from some association with that party. Jesus himself was, however, far removed from their attitudes, even though he was charged with inciting rebellion and died the same death as many of the Zealots.

The *Essenes* were members of a movement which drew aside from the mainstream of Jewish life, originally in protest against the uniting of supreme religious, as well as civil and military, power in the hands of the Hasmoneans. Most of the Essenes lived in the towns and villages of Judea. Some, perhaps a dissident group, lived in the monastery recently discovered at Qumran on the Dead Sea. At Qumran, the Essenes worked and prayed, living a common life in poverty and celibacy. One of their most notable features was a scrupulous attention to ritual purity and the taking of frequent baths.

From their writings which were discovered at Qumran after 1947 ("the Dead Sea Scrolls"), a great deal is known about their beliefs. They saw themselves as a faithful remnant gathered together by "the teacher of righteousness," expiating the sins of their people while they awaited the arrival of a new age in which Israel would be purified and restored under the leadership of a prophet like Moses, a messiah descended from David, and a high priest of the line of Aaron. Like the early Christians, they regarded recent and contemporary events as fulfillments of prophecies made in the Scriptures.

There are similarities between the Essene movement and early Christianity, and Essenism illustrates the hopes and expectations which Jesus came to fulfill. The difference between the two is, however, very great. Principally it is the person and mission of Jesus, his teaching and his death and resurrection.

Jesus of Nazareth does indeed belong to the world into which he is born. He is not foreign to it and can only be properly understood within it. And yet within that world he is unique and finally he transcends it.

For Study or Discussion

1. "By the time Jesus was born, the world was ready for his coming." In what ways?
2. Are we fair to the Pharisees?
3. "Judaism and Christianity are sisters who quarreled." Discuss this.

15

The Good News

The Good News of Jesus Christ ◊ **The Preaching of the Apostles** ◊
The Gospel Story ◊ **The Four Gospels** ◊ **Matthew** ◊ **Mark** ◊ **Luke**
◊ **John** ◊ **The Gospels and Jesus**

The Good News of Jesus Christ

The "Gospel" (an old English word meaning "good news") is "the good news of Jesus Christ the Son of God" (Mk 1:1). Jesus himself wrote no books. During his brief public ministry he went about mainly in Galilee but also in Judea and occasionally in pagan territory, teaching by word of mouth. The heart of his teaching was the announcement that the kingdom of God was close at hand and even now breaking in. This was the good news. He called on his hearers to repent and believe the "Gospel" (see Mk 1:14–15).

Jesus also healed the sick, drove out evil spirits and worked other miracles as signs that the kingdom of God was already coming into the world. As well as that, he taught people about the kingdom of God, what it is like, how to enter it. In his teaching, he made use of ways of thinking and explaining things which would strike his hearers and which they would remember. One of Jesus' favorite methods of teaching was the parable, in which, using everyday situations—farming, fishing, the home, politics—he tried to get his hearers to see themselves and their relationships with God and with one another in a new light.

Our Lord not only told people about the kingdom of God. He

actually brought the kingdom into the world. By the death and resurrection of Jesus, the power of Satan was breached and the means of victory given. God began to reign over the human race.

The Preaching of the Apostles

During his public life Jesus gathered about him a chosen band of followers, the twelve. They heard what he said and saw what he did, and so were able to tell others. They even had a share in his ministry. Jesus sent them out to proclaim the good news of the coming of God's kingdom and gave them power to heal the sick and drive out demons as signs that the kingdom was here.

After Pentecost, the Church proclaimed that the kingdom of God had been brought into the world through the death and resurrection of Jesus. As St. Peter declared: "God raised this man Jesus to life and all of us are witnesses to that. . . . For this reason the whole house of Israel can be certain that God has made this Jesus whom you crucified both Lord and Christ" (Acts 2:32, 36).

This was the good news which the apostles and their companions preached everywhere, to Jews and pagans, and confirmed with miracles (as we read in the Acts of the Apostles). They called on their hearers to repent and believe in the Lord Jesus and in the salvation he had won by his death and resurrection.

The Gospel Story

The apostles and their followers did not present these truths in a dry, abstract way. They told a story, the story of the life, death and resurrection of Jesus. It was a story which they themselves now understood more fully with the assistance of the Holy Spirit.

The purpose of telling this story was not simply to give interesting biographical information about Jesus. Peter and the others wanted to convert people and win them to faith in Christ, and so they told what they had seen and heard. Theirs was a true story, and the faith they proclaimed was in a real person and in real events.

The Gospel story took shape as it was told and retold under the guidance of the Holy Spirit. The passion was always told in a fairly standard form. On the other hand, the accounts of what Jesus taught and did in his public ministry, beginning with his baptism in the Jordan, were more varied.

Which of the many sayings and deeds of Jesus were passed on and how they were presented would depend to a large extent on the capacity, interests and needs of the hearers. Certain ones constantly found a place. Even so, they were not always told in an identical manner. After all, one saying or one incident could be capable of being applied in more than one way, thus meeting the requirements of rather different groups of people.

An instructive example of this is the parable of the lost sheep, which is told in two Gospels. In Luke (15:4–7) the story of the shepherd who leaves the ninety-nine sheep to go off in search of the single stray is told in order to justify Jesus' habit of welcoming sinners and eating with them, to the scandal of the "virtuous." The joy of the shepherd at finding the lost sheep is emphasized, and the point is made: "In the same way, I tell you, there will be more rejoicing in heaven over one repentant sinner than over ninety-nine virtuous men who have no need of repentance." Told this way, the story probably reflects the situation of Jesus' own life and ministry.

In Matthew (18:12–14) the same story is told for the benefit of those called to have authority in the community of Jesus' followers and who are to have special care of "the little ones." This time the point is: "Similarly, it is never the will of your Father in heaven that one of these little ones should be lost." Told this way, the story probably reflects the situation of the early Church.

For the most part, the Gospel story was handed on by word of mouth and committed to memory. No doubt, however, memory was assisted by written collections of sayings, parables and miracle stories.

The Four Gospels

Eventually the four pamphlets which we know as the Gospels of Matthew, Mark, Luke and John were composed. They are named after two apostles (Matthew and John) and two who were disciples of the apostles (Mark, of Peter and Paul, and Luke, of

Paul). Each of them, no doubt, did play a vital part in the forma-
tion of "his" Gospel, so that there is a real sense in which it can
be named after him. But this may not have meant that he was
responsible for the Gospel as we have it. In some cases, at least,
the evangelist whose name the Gospel bears may have been responsible for an earlier stage of its composition, or may even stand
at the head of the tradition from which the Gospel eventually
emerged.

Scholars are not agreed as to the order in which the Gospels
were written or the dates of their composition or the relations between them. Traditionally it was held that the first Gospel to appear was written by Matthew the apostle in Aramaic and later
translated into Greek. In recent times the usual opinion has been
that Mark's was the first Gospel and that, along with a collection
of sayings of Jesus (referred to as "Q") which has since disappeared, it was used by both Matthew and Luke in the composition
of their Gospels. Other scholars believe that Matthew and even
Luke are earlier than Mark.

In fact the relations of the Gospels to one another seem to be
very complex. Matthew, Mark and Luke obviously have a great
deal in common. They even seem to have borrowed from one another. But who borrowed from whom? Are Matthew and Luke
long versions of Mark, or is Mark a short version of Matthew and
Luke? And what about John? Did the author of the fourth Gospel
know the other three? We have just seen that the process by
which our Gospels came into being involved a number of stages.
It could well be that during the formative period, several independent written accounts of Jesus' life and teaching were in circulation and influenced one another in various ways, until they
crystallized in the four Gospels as we have them now. The Gospels
of Matthew, Mark and Luke seem to have undergone a process of
harmonization which worked in the direction of producing agreement among them and perhaps would have eventually produced
a single unified Gospel. The fourth Gospel seems to have some
connections with the other three, and in particular with that of
Luke, but it has a different history.

Here we shall discuss the four Gospels in the order in which
they are found in the New Testament. As for the dates of com-

position, we shall take it that Mark at least was written in the 60's, and that Matthew and Luke were in existence either before or after A.D. 70 (depending on whether one thinks they do or do not presuppose that the temple of Jerusalem has already been destroyed). John we will place, with early Church tradition, toward the end of the century, in the 90's. It should be noticed that, on this dating, there was at least one of our four Gospels in circulation within thirty years or so of the events narrated—within the lifetime, therefore, of contemporaries of those events. This is an important point in favor of the reliability of the Gospels.

All four Gospels have a similar structure, which they inherited from the original preaching of the good news by the apostles. In each Gospel, the final section, dealing with the events of Holy Week, forms a large proportion of the whole: in John, about half, in Mark, about one-third. This is preceded by a narrative of the public ministry of Jesus, what he said and did as he went about in Palestine.

Matthew, Mark and Luke are called the "Synoptic Gospels" because they often parallel one another and so can be "seen together." These three give a similar picture of the ministry of Jesus. It took place mainly in Galilee, with short excursions to neighboring districts. Then followed the journey to Jerusalem, the entry into the holy city, a brief ministry in Jerusalem, and finally the passion and resurrection. The whole public life of Jesus, according to the Synoptic Gospels, might have lasted only one year. John gives quite a different picture. In the course of the fourth Gospel, Jesus makes several journeys to Jerusalem for the Jewish feasts, and his ministry takes place not only in Galilee and the north, but in Judea and the south, and also in Samaria. Three separate Passovers are celebrated, including the one during which Jesus suffered, so that, according to John, the public ministry would have lasted at least two to three years.

Matthew, Luke and John introduce their Gospels with an explanation of who Jesus is and where he came from. Matthew and Luke tell us that he was conceived by the Holy Spirit and born of the Virgin Mary, and they also hand on stories of the childhood of Jesus and of his upbringing at Nazareth. These "infancy narratives" are different in tone and style from the rest of the Gospels of Matthew and Luke. They are full of references to the Old Testament, and whole sections seem to have been written with the Jewish Scriptures in mind, e.g., the annunciation (Lk 1:26–38) which recalls the commissioning of Gideon to perform a great work on behalf of the Lord (Jgs 6:11–24). Right from the outset Matthew and Luke want to establish Jesus as the fulfillment of the expectations of Israel, Matthew through the genealogy with which he traces Jesus' descent from Abraham and David, and Luke through three songs—of Mary (the Magnificat), of Zechariah (the Benedictus), and of Simeon (the Nunc Dimittis).

John goes back even further than Matthew and Luke. He tells us that Jesus, who is the Word of God, was with God in the beginning, in fact that he was God. Mark, by contrast, abruptly states that "Jesus came from Nazareth in Galilee and was baptized in the Jordan by John" (1:9).

Matthew

The Gospel can be seen as a new torah. This is clear even from the type of literature it is. Each of the Gospels, in its combination of story and instruction, recalls the Books of Exodus and Numbers. The resemblance to the torah is most obvious in Matthew. There the ministry of Jesus—between the accounts of his infancy (chapters 1–2) and his passion and resurrection (chapters 26–28)—is presented in the form of five sections, recalling the "five books of Moses," the Pentateuch or torah. Each of these sections consists of a narrative telling part of the ministry of Jesus followed by a long speech in which Jesus sets out his teaching.

The first section (chapters 3 and 4) contains the beginning of Jesus' ministry of teaching and healing. Then follows the Sermon on the Mount (chapters 5–7) which has been called "the charter of the kingdom of heaven" (the "mountain" where Jesus gave his instruction recalls, of course, Mount Sinai where God gave the torah). The law of Jesus begins with the beatitudes, as the law of Moses begins with the ten commandments, and goes on to spell out the behavior and even the inward attitudes of those who belong to the kingdom. The second section begins with ten miracles of Jesus (chapters 8–9) and continues with his special instructions to the twelve before sending them out on mission (chapter 10). In the third section the story of Jesus' ministry is carried forward (chapters 11–12); then follows a series of parables telling what the kingdom of heaven is like (chapter 13), beginning with the parable of the sower which Mark and Luke also have.

In the fourth section we reach the turning point of Jesus' ministry in Galilee and the north: the feeding of the crowd in the desert, Peter's acknowledgement of Jesus as Messiah, Jesus' prediction of his passion, and the transfiguration (chapters 14–17). In chapter 18 Jesus gives instructions about the community of those who follow him and believe in him. The fifth section narrates the journey to Jerusalem, the entry into the holy city and the ministry there (chapters 19–23) and concludes with Jesus' teaching on the end—on the end of Jerusalem and of the world, on the coming of the Son of Man and on the judgment (chapters 24–25). The last three chapters bring the story of Jesus to an end and a new beginning.

The theme throughout Matthew's Gospel is the kingdom of heaven, that is, the reign of God over those who acknowledge his kingship. This kingdom was prepared in Israel and has been established by Jesus through his teaching and his miracles, and especially through his death and resurrection. Matthew often shows how the Scriptures have been fulfilled by Jesus. In fact, many features of his Gospel are written for people of Jewish background. In his account of the public ministry, he portrays Jesus as the Teacher instructing the people about the kingdom and forming those who are to spread the good news of the kingdom throughout the world. Matthew's Jesus is also the New Moses, spokesman of God and leader of his people in the new exodus which was so eagerly expected.

Mark

Mark is deceptive. He is simple, direct and brief (this is by far the shortest of the Gospels). However, there is nothing primitive about either his artistry or his theology. He tells his story with bold strokes and occasional vivid details, many of which may have come originally from an eyewitness (whom early Church tradition would identify as St Peter, whose assistant Mark was at Rome).

Mark's Gospel has pace, tension and drama. For that reason, and also because it is comparatively short, it can be read at one sitting (with, perhaps, a break after chapter 9, verse 1). Such a continuous reading is amply worthwhile. It enables the Gospel story and its message to stand out. The outline of the public life of Jesus, which Mark has in common with Matthew and Luke, is clear: the baptism in the Jordan and the temptation in the wilderness (chapter 1); the ministry in Galilee and elsewhere in the north, with headquarters at Capernaum on the lakeside (chapters 2–9); the journey to Jerusalem (chapter 10); the ministry in Jerusalem before Passover (chapters 11–13); the passion and resurrection (chapters 14–16).

Dramatically, the Gospel of Mark falls into two roughly equal "acts." Act I has a prologue (the baptism) and builds up to a climax in chapter 8 with Peter's acknowledgment of Jesus as Messiah and the prediction of the passion. Act I ends with the words of Jesus: "I tell you solemnly, there are some standing here who will not taste death before they see the kingdom of God coming with power" (9:1). Act II opens with another prologue (the transfiguration—a first fulfillment of the prediction in 9:1 and a clear parallel to the baptism) and builds up to the crisis of Calvary. Act II ends with the resurrection of Jesus, which is the coming of the kingdom of God with power.

From Mark's Gospel there emerges the fascinating figure of Jesus, a person of tremendous and mysterious power who compels us, as he compelled his contemporaries, to ask: Who is this man? We see him boldly challenge and attack the domination of the evil spirits. The powers of darkness counterattack through human agents—the Jewish leaders and the Roman authorities—and appear to win on Calvary. But on the cross Jesus is finally recognized as Son of God, and the resurrection turns his defeat into victory.

Luke

Many touches in the third Gospel show the special interest of a non-Jewish convert from paganism writing for others like himself—the sort of person tradition says St. Luke was. The first two chapters are devoted to the birth and childhood of Jesus. Then from chapter 3 onward, Luke follows the same general outline as Mark. However, he includes a great deal of material not found in Mark, most notably a long section (9:51 to 18:14) which he sets within the context of the journey to Jerusalem (compare Mk 10:1). The two Gospels come together again at Mark 10:13 and Luke 18:15.

A large proportion of the material in Luke which is not in Mark is, however, found in Matthew, though not always in the same place in the Gospel or in an identical form. Thus Luke has a "Sermon on the Plain" (6:17–49) which has much in common with Matthew's "Sermon on the Mount" and occurs at about the same point in the Gospel. His version of the beatitudes is, however, somewhat different from Matthew's. Furthermore, items of Jesus' teaching which Matthew includes in the Sermon on the Mount are given by Luke not in the Sermon on the Plain but elsewhere in his Gospel—the Lord's Prayer in 11:1–4 and the instruction on trust in the providence of God who feeds the birds and clothes the flowers in 12:22–32.

St. Luke has been called "the scribe of the gentleness of Christ." His is the Gospel of the "little ones," the outcasts of society, both civil and religious. It is the Gospel of the poor, with some hard things to say about the rich (Jesus' gentleness is not weakness). It is the Gospel of prayer and of the Holy Spirit. It is the Gospel of women, especially of the Virgin Mary.

Luke alone has some of the greatest of Jesus' stories: the good Samaritan (10:29–37), the prodigal son (15:11–32), the rich man and Lazarus (16:19–31), the Pharisee and the publican (18:9–14). It is in this Gospel that we see Jesus in the home of Martha and Mary (10:38–42) and of Zacchaeus the reformed tax collector (19:1–10). The crucified Jesus prays for the forgiveness of his murderers and promises paradise to the repentant thief (23:33–43). Luke's is, above all, the Gospel of the all-embracing mercy of God.

John

At first sight the fourth Gospel seems to be very different from the other three. We have already seen that it gives a quite different impression of the length of Jesus' public ministry and even of where it took place. In John as in the others, the ministry of Jesus is one of teaching and healing, and it reaches a turning point with the feeding of the crowd in the desert and Peter's acknowledgment of Jesus. However, for the most part the incidents of the ministry in John are not the same as those in Matthew, Mark and Luke.

John's account of these incidents is remarkably precise in determining times and places—in contrast to the Synoptics, who are often vague about such matters. Other details, too, are realistic and full of life and seem to show close acquaintance with the events and their setting. This setting is not only the country and its people. It is also the Jewish religion, its liturgy and its Scriptures. John's is a deeply Jewish Gospel.

Another notable difference between John and the other Gospels lies in the long speeches which Jesus makes in the fourth Gospel. These seem to be unlike anything in the Synoptics, where by and large Jesus makes quite brief statements, and even the longer speeches seem often to be made up of a series of pithy sayings which were probably handed down by the tradition as isolated units and strung together by the evangelists. In John there are hardly any parables, which are such a feature of the Synoptics. Even the topics about which Jesus speaks are different: in John it is typically his own person and mission. Finally, the tone of these speeches in the fourth Gospel is different and conveys an atmosphere of mystery.

Closer inspection reveals, however, that many points in the speeches of Jesus in John are linked with things he says in the Synoptic Gospels, for instance, the teaching about the good shepherd in John 10:1–16 with the parable of the lost sheep in Matthew and Luke. This has led many scholars to think that the speeches in John are developments of briefer sayings of Jesus which are either in the Synoptic Gospels or were handed down by independent tradition. Long reflection under the inspiration of the Holy Spirit would have discovered deeper meanings and wider implications in them, and these are drawn out and expressed in the fourth Gospel.

Of course, in his preaching and teaching Jesus would normally have spoken at much greater length than anything in the Gospels. All of them, the Synoptics as well as John, were attempting to hand on the essence of what Jesus had said as this had come down to them. There is more than one way of doing this: not only by repeating characteristic sayings but also by unpacking the meanings which often lie below the surface. John also emphasizes features which are in the Synoptics but not so prominently, such as the relationship between Jesus and his Father.

The Gospel of John opens with a prologue (1:1–18) which recalls the first chapter of the Book of Genesis, not only the "In the beginning" and the creative Word of God, but also "life," "light" and "darkness," which are key words in the Gospel. Overtones of Genesis, especially of the opening chapters, continue throughout the Gospel: the garden, the man and the woman, the water of life, the tree of life. In Jesus there is a new creation.

After his baptism, the ministry of Jesus begins in Galilee (1:19–2:12). Then follows a first visit to Jerusalem for Passover and a brief ministry in Judea (2:13–3:36). Jesus goes to Samaria (4:1–42) on his way back to Galilee (4:43–54). He goes again to Jerusalem for a festival and cures a sick man at the pool of Bethzatha (chapter 5). Once more in Galilee at the lakeside (chapter 6) Jesus feeds the crowd, resists an attempt to make him king, walks on the water, teaches in the synagogue at Capernaum on the bread of life, and receives the declaration of Peter: "You have the message of eternal life, and we believe; we know that you are the Holy One of God" (6:68–69). There follows a further period of ministry centered on Jerusalem and lasting several months which reaches a climax with the raising of Lazarus (chapters 7–11). The events of the last Passover are told at length (chapters 12–20). The last chapter (21) seems to have been added as a kind of appendix.

St. John is traditionally called "the Theologian." He soars to the heights, like the eagle which is his emblem. He shows us Jesus as the Word of God made flesh who has come into the world to continue the work of his Father and bring us life and light. In his passion Jesus is the King. And yet it is the same Jesus who sits down weary at the well of Samaria, and who weeps for Lazarus his friend. For John too, Jesus fulfills the Scriptures. Powerful symbols from the Old Testament—bread, water, the lamb, the vine, the temple, the shepherd—show that in Jesus God has kept his word once given to Israel.

The Gospels and Jesus

The Gospel writers were concerned, as St. Luke puts it, to "draw up their accounts of the events which have taken place among us, exactly as they were handed down to us by those who from the outset were eyewitnesses and ministers of the word" (1:1–2). However, notwithstanding their fidelity to tradition and their care to transmit it exactly, they were no mere scissors-and-paste editors. Each of them is not only a great theologian but also a great artist. Each transmits the tradition, but in his own way. What we have is the good news of Jesus Christ, but it is the good news according to Matthew, Mark, Luke and John. Each therefore presents a somewhat different facet or aspect of the person and work of Jesus. All four, however, faithfully hand on what he really did and taught for our salvation.

The four Gospels are like four portraits of the same person made by four different artists. Each has seen something different in the subject and seeks to present it in his own way. The comparison is perhaps even closer if we think of the portraits as paintings rather than as photographs. Painters are allowed a certain freedom in the composition of their pictures. They are able to arrange their data so as to arrive at a result that may not correspond exactly to any photograph which might be taken. For all that, the painter can often reveal a deeper truth about the subject than would appear in a photograph.

In a somewhat similar way, the four evangelists have used a certain freedom in the composition of their Gospels. They have arranged their data so as to produce four different portraits of Jesus which are, so to say, "paintings" rather than "photographs." They are, however, true likenesses of Jesus and are able to reveal depths of meaning in his person and in his work which might not be obvious at first sight.

For Study or Discussion

1. Go through the Song of the Virgin Mary (the Magnificat), Luke 1:46–55, and the Song of Zechariah (the Benedictus), Luke 1:67–79, and point out the various Old Testament themes which occur.

2. What is the Gospel?

3. How did the Church get on before the Gospels were written?

4. Are the Gospels true?

5. Which of the four Gospels do you find most appealing? Why?

16

Spreading the Gospel

The Acts of the Apostles is a sequel to St. Luke's Gospel (compare the opening verses of each book). Both together form a history in two parts of the origins of the Christian Church. The Book of Acts was written to show how the apostles and the first followers of Jesus witnessed to him and proclaimed his Gospel "not only in Jerusalem but throughout Judea and Samaria, and indeed to the ends of the earth" (1:8).

In his second volume, as in his first, Luke draws on earlier sources. These included traditions, some of them probably written down, about events, persons and missionary activities, which stemmed from the churches of Jerusalem and Antioch. Luke also had St. Paul's story of his conversion and missionary journeys, and his own travel log kept while accompanying Paul on some of them.

All this material Luke made into a connected narrative. He seems to have had in mind several different types of literature current at the time which he used as models, including the travel story, the biography, and the general history. The title "Acts of . . ." is familiar from secular literature of the time for a book describing the deeds and achievements of someone. There is no doubt, however, that the book which most deeply influenced St. Luke was the Bible, i.e., the Old Testament in the ancient Greek translation known as the Septuagint, which is constantly echoed in both the contents and the style of Acts.

In organizing his material, Luke made use of a time scale which stretches from the Ascension of Christ (about A.D. 30) into the 60's. However, a great deal is left vague in dating various events and relating them to one another in time. Gaps in the time scale are frequently filled by bridge passages which summarize a state of affairs and move the story on to the next stage.

Luke seems to have treated his sources with great respect, extending as far as the language and style in which they were originally couched. Where details of things like the local civic organization of towns in Asia Minor can be checked, they appear to show first-hand knowledge of those places around the middle of the first century. These features count in favor of the general historical reliability of Acts. All the same, it is fair to say that throughout the book, Luke is not writing history for its own sake but rather using history to illustrate his theme, which is the triumphal progress of the Gospel. It also seems that Luke's work was later re-edited by another hand.

The Book of Acts contains a number of sermons and addresses. As with other ancient historians, Luke probably wrote what he considered to be appropriate speeches to place on the lips of his speakers. However, these would not have been simply free compositions. Like the Greek historian Thucydides (who explains his method), Luke would have used sources for these speeches when they were available—his own or others' reminiscences, even perhaps written summaries taken down at the time. It is especially noteworthy that in the first sermons of St. Peter (e.g., 2:14–36), the manner in which the death and resurrection of Jesus are proclaimed, and even the language which is used, appear to reflect faithfully the earliest Christian preaching of the Gospel.

Luke's insight into character and human nature, as well as his ability to write a gripping story, are factors which make the Acts of the Apostles good reading. Luke emerges as an educated and observant man, as much at home in the world of Greek-speaking Judaism as in the pagan world into which he was probably born, a sympathetic spirit and a fit person to describe how the good news of Jesus Christ reached Antioch, Athens and Rome, the great centers of the civilized world.

Despite its title, the Acts of the Apostles does not describe the careers of all the apostles, but mainly of two, St. Peter and St. Paul. In the first half of the book, the leading figure is Peter. We read first of the birth of the Church in Jerusalem at Pentecost and of its early life and growth (chapters 1–5). Then comes the spread of the Gospel—despite or even because of persecution—throughout Judea and Samaria and beyond, and the conversion of the first non-Jewish believers (chapters 6–12). The good news has now reached Antioch, capital of Syria and third city of the Roman empire, which becomes a second center of the young Church and of its missionary endeavor.

Attention shifts to St Paul. He has already been introduced as an accomplice in the martyrdom of Stephen (chapter 7), and we have learned of his conversion on the road to Damascus (chapter 9). Now we read about his first missionary journey through Cyprus and parts of what today is Turkey (chapters 13–14).

Controversy breaks out in the early Church about whether converts from paganism are obliged to observe the whole Jewish law, in other words, to become Jews in order to become Christians. The meeting of "apostles and elders" at Jerusalem decides that they are not, and so opens the door wide to non-Jews (chapter 15). This was one of the most significant steps taken by the Church in that or in any age. Not only did it make Christianity accessible to many more people. It also defined the Church as more than a movement within Judaism and began a gradual parting of the ways which would end in total separation.

Paul himself was an advocate of the "open door" policy. In his own missionary work, however, he generally preached first to Jews and only then to non-Jews. Furthermore, the non-Jews to whom he preached the Gospel were usually not out-and-out pagans, but pagans who were sympathetic to Judaism. They accepted the Jews' belief in one God and their high moral code, but were reluctant to submit themselves to all the prescriptions of the law. Such people readily welcomed the message of Paul and embraced Christianity in growing numbers. St. Luke himself was probably one of them.

It is therefore no coincidence that the map of the early expansion of the Christian Church closely resembles the map of the Jewish diaspora. Quite simply, the Jewish communities with their

Gentile adherents spread throughout the Mediterranean world and in Mesopotamia were the natural targets for the missionary endeavor of the early Church. The synagogues gave Paul and others a platform and an audience.

Chapters 16–20 of Acts describe two further missionary journeys of St. Paul in Turkey and also in Greece. On one of them he visited Athens, the cultural capital of the Mediterranean world, where he departed from his usual practice and preached directly to a pagan audience (chapter 17). During at least part of these missions, Luke himself was his companion. Chapters 21–28 tell how Paul was arrested in Jerusalem, how he used his rights as a Roman citizen to appeal to the emperor, and so came to Rome, where he continued even as a prisoner to preach the Gospel.

The Book of Acts ends there. The good news of Jesus Christ has reached Rome, capital of the Empire. The year was A.D. 63, and it seems that the book was probably written not long after. St. Paul himself died a martyr in Rome about A.D. 67.

Shortly after that, Jerusalem fell to the Romans. Many Christians had already left the city while there was still time. That was the end of the church of Jerusalem described in the Book of Acts. Christians of Jewish origin, observing all or part of the law, still existed. However, relations with the sister religion worsened, and eventually they were forbidden entry into the synagogues which, after the destruction of the Jerusalem temple in A.D. 70, were the centers of Jewish spiritual and communal life. The Christian community had decided that it was not necessary to be both a Jew and a Christian. Now the Jewish community decided that it was not possible to be both a Jew and a Christian.

In the meantime, non-Jewish or Gentile Christianity continued to grow in strength and became the predominant and finally the only type of Christianity.

In the course of his story of the spread of the Gospel, St. Luke portrays the life of the newborn Church. He is interested in its liturgy—the celebration of baptism and the Eucharist—and in its organization—the twelve and the seven in Jerusalem, prophets and teachers in Antioch, elders in Jerusalem and the new churches founded by Paul and Barnabas.

In places, no doubt, the picture of the Church drawn by Luke is somewhat idealized. On the other hand, he does not disguise that there were tensions: between "Hebrews" and "Hellenists" (Christian Jews of Palestinian and non-Palestinian origin respectively); between the churches of Jerusalem and Antioch; between those who believed that in order to become Christians it was necessary also to become Jews and those who did not. One of the lessons of the book is that, even with diversity and disagreement, it is possible to build unity.

Furthermore, the cameo portraits of the Jerusalem community, "united heart and soul," owning all property in common, and "remaining faithful to the teaching of the apostles, to the brotherhood, to the breaking of bread and to the prayers" (2:42–47 and 4:32–35), will always provide Christians with a challenging image of the Church they might be.

Throughout the book, St. Luke draws attention to the direction and guidance of the Holy Spirit. The Holy Spirit is seen to intervene especially at the turning points of the work of spreading the Gospel—such as Peter's reception of Cornelius (chapter 10) and Paul's decision to cross over from Asia to Europe (16:6–10)—prompting people to go further and to take steps which they would not otherwise have taken and which were even against their natural inclination. The Church is thus presented as more than a human project. In fact the spread of the Gospel and the growth of the Church are portrayed as the effects of the descent of the Holy Spirit at Pentecost. This book could just as well be called "The Acts of the Holy Spirit."

For Study or Discussion

1. Show how Acts 1:8 states a program which is worked out in the rest of the Book of Acts.
2. "The Acts of the Apostles is the first history of the Church." How correct is this description?
3. What points can you find in common between St. Luke's Gospel and the Acts of the Apostles?
4. This book could just as well be called "The Acts of the Holy Spirit." Does this description say something true and important about the Book of Acts?

17

Early Christian Letters

Letters in the New Testament ◊ Letter Writing in the Ancient World ◊ The Letters of Paul ◊ The Letter to the Hebrews ◊ Letters to All the Churches ◊ Unity and Diversity

Letters in the New Testament

After the Acts of the Apostles comes a collection of letters (or epistles, as they are also called). Thirteen of them are written by or in the name of St. Paul, one (to the Hebrews) carries no author's name but has traditionally been grouped with St. Paul's, one has the name of St. James, two of St. Peter, three of St. John, and one of St. Jude. Other letters are contained in longer books of the New Testament (Acts and Revelation).

Scholars argue about whether all these letters were actually written by those whose names they bear. The question is complicated. In all probability, none of the authors would have sat down and personally written a letter in his own hand. It was the usual thing in those days to dictate to a secretary. Often, in fact, the "author" simply gave the secretary an idea of the sort of thing the letter was about and left it to the secretary to draft—something we are familiar with in office procedure today. The wording of the letter, even perhaps the detail of the ideas, would therefore be the secretary's. It was still, however, a letter from the person whose name it bore and whose message it conveyed. It follows that if one author used several secretaries, a series of letters could differ noticeably among themselves. A further complication in the case of

133

Paul is that some of his letters bear several names as co-senders and possibly in some sense as co-authors. One must also allow for the fact that over the years, style, vocabulary and ideas can all change. All the same, many scholars would claim that in the case of some of the New Testament letters, an anonymous Christian, perhaps a disciple of one of the apostles, has issued a letter in his name expressing what it is supposed he would have thought.

In the ancient world, and indeed until the invention of the telegraph and the telephone, letters were the only means of long-distance communication. The Roman empire had an excellent system of roads and also river and sea transport. So it was criss-crossed by the best system of communication known until modern times, a system which linked the Middle East, North Africa, Western Europe, the Balkans and Turkey. There was, however, no state postal service, or at least none that was available to the private citizen, so letter writers had to make their own arrangements with messengers. It is clear from the New Testament letters themselves that the messenger was meant also to convey a message by word of mouth which explained the letter or which the letter itself supported. The same sources, and the Acts of the Apostles, reveal that the early Christians made full use of the means of communication available to them.

Letter Writing in the Ancient World

A great many letters have come down to us from the ancient world. The majority are brief personal or business communications. Others are much longer and more elaborately composed, generally with an eye to publication. In some cases the letter form has simply been used as a vehicle for conveying ideas to a wide audience, where a modern writer would publish an article or an essay. Letters were also used to publish laws and convey legal decisions.

As with us, certain conventions of addressing and signing letters were observed. We begin our letters (whether to a close friend or to a perfect stranger) with "Dear so-and-so," and we end up "Yours sincerely (or faithfully, or cordially)" and our name. In the ancient world, a letter began with the name of the sender, then "to so-and-so," followed by a greeting word such as "peace" or "health." Next there was often a prayer of good wishes for the welfare of the recipient (like our "I trust this finds you well"). The letter ended with a word of farewell, which was as a rule written by the sender in his or her own hand and served as a signature and a mark of authentication.

All these features apply to the New Testament letters. Most of them are true letters sent by a named person or persons to an individual or a community. Three of them, St. Paul's Letter to Philemon and the Second and Third Letters of John, are about the standard length of personal letters in the ancient world. Most, however, are considerably longer. Often they contain the sorts of personal items that would be found in ordinary correspondence— messages, greetings, information. In general, however, they are used as vehicles for instruction about Christian beliefs and practices and for encouragement and warning. As a result, the New Testament letters are weightier documents than the personal and business letters that have survived from the ancient world.

Some of the letters, e.g., Paul's two letters to the Christians of Corinth, form part of a two-way correspondence of which we possess only one side (and, it seems, not the whole of that either). This must be borne in mind in reading these letters and trying to understand them. It is rather like listening to only one side of a telephone conversation, so that one misses the point of a great deal that is said. Most of St. Paul's letters, in fact, were written in view of a particular state of affairs at one time and place or to answer specific questions put to him.

Other New Testament letters, such as that of James, give the impression of being more like essays intended for publication and written at leisure to set out certain ideas of the author before a general readership. St. Paul, too, seems to be aware that at least some of his letters, even though written to a particular group of people, and with them and their situation and problems very much in mind, would in fact circulate more widely. There is also an example in the New Testament of a letter which was a legal document used to convey the decision of a law-making body. It is

given in full in Acts 15:23–29, and communicates the ruling of
the so-called "Council of Jerusalem" in terms similar to those used
by the Roman emperor and governors in giving legal judgments.

   This last mentioned letter begins in due form, "The apostles
and elders, your brothers, to the brothers of pagan origin in Antioch, Syria and Cilicia, send greetings," and ends with the word
"Farewell." Most of the letters of the New Testament observe the
conventions of beginning and ending letters, usually, however,
with some variation on the bare essentials. St. Paul, in particular,
likes to develop the greeting into an elaborate paragraph (see, for
instance, Rom 1:1–8, which is a theological statement in itself)
and follows it with a blessing and prayer which can also be quite
lengthy (see especially Eph 1:3–23). Paul usually finishes his letters with a sentence or two in his own hand, simply to serve as a
farewell, or sometimes to guarantee the genuineness of the letter
or to underscore his message (see Col 4:18; 2 Thes 3:17–18; Gal
6:11–18). Others of the New Testament letters, however, have no
greeting or no farewell—consider, for example, the Letter to the
Hebrews (no greeting, but a farewell) and the First Letter of St.
John (no greeting and no farewell).

The Letters of Paul

   The letters of St Paul are grouped roughly in the order of their
length. They are addressed to the Christians in Rome, Corinth
(two letters), Galatia (in central Asia Minor or Turkey), Ephesus,
Philippi, Colossae, and Thessalonica (two letters), and to certain
individuals, Timothy (two letters), Titus, and Philemon. The earliest of them to be written were the Letters to the Thessalonians
(A.D. 50–52), which are, therefore, the first New Testament writings. The other letters were written through the 50's and 60's.

   Despite the fact that they are written to particular people and
deal with specific topics of concern to Paul and his readers, these
letters were from the first regarded as of more than passing interest. For one thing, they bear the name of the great apostle. The
matters they deal with are usually central to Christian belief and
practice, and so, if some passages strike us today as not particu-
larly relevant, many others have remained and still are highly top-

ical. The reader is impressed, moved and convinced by the sheer authority of Paul and by his warmth and urgency. He is a master of words. He has the knack of coining striking and memorable phrases, and some of his longer passages, such as Romans 8:31–39 and 1 Corinthians 13:1–13, would rank among the noblest words ever written.

The Acts of the Apostles provides us with a good deal of background information to the letters of Paul, and the letters themselves fill out the portrait of this extraordinary man, a Jew born outside Palestine who became first an ardent member of the Pharisee party and then gave himself totally to Christ and to the preaching of the good news. Paul's letters breathe the spirit of the apostle of the Gentiles as we get to know him in the Book of Acts: a man of action yet a thinker and a speaker, with deep and strong emotions but also a keen and daring intellect, the sort of man who can dedicate himself completely to a cause and yet have a marked sensitivity and tenderness.

The same Book of Acts also gives us the foundation of the whole of St. Paul's preaching and writing. It was his experience on the road to Damascus: "There came a light from heaven all round him. He fell to the ground, and then he heard a voice saying, 'Saul, Saul, why are you persecuting me?' 'Who are you, Lord?' he asked, and the voice answered, 'I am Jesus, and you are persecuting me. Get up now and go into the city, and you will be told what you have to do' " (Acts 9: 3–6). From this experience Paul learned that the Jesus whose followers he was persecuting has been raised from the dead and that he lives in those who believe in him. In the same moment Paul also understood that Jesus forgives us even while we are still his enemies. During the rest of his life Paul continued to deepen his understanding of these truths and to expound them in speech and in writing. For on the road to Damascus he learned too that he himself had been called and chosen to work for the Lord as his apostle.

The resurrection of Christ is a frequent theme in St Paul's letters. He often writes of Christ's resurrection and relates it to us. We will rise with Christ in the resurrection on the last day (see 1 Thes 4:13–18; 1 Cor 15). Indeed we have already been raised with Christ from death to new life in baptism (Rom 6:1–14).

The Church as the body of Christ—especially through the Eucharist—is one of the leading ideas in 1 Corinthians, where St. Paul stresses the need for unity and cooperation among "members" (literally "limbs" or "organs") of the body. In the Letters to the Ephesians and the Colossians, the emphasis is rather on the unity and identity between head and members—the Church is the "completion" of Christ.

We cannot earn God's love, but must accept it as a free gift by faith in Christ. That is the main theme of the Letters to the Romans and the Galatians. In Galatians also, St. Paul asserts that he has received his appointment as an apostle personally from Christ, and in Chapters 10–12 of 2 Corinthians he describes what being an apostle has meant for him, namely, continual labors and sufferings.

In all his letters, St. Paul points out the consequences of the Christian faith in terms of our moral and spiritual lives. To be "in Christ" is to be a "new creation," no longer living according to the dictates of the "flesh" but following the promptings of the Spirit.

St. Paul's thought is not always easy to follow, and he can be seriously misunderstood—as is pointed out in the Second Letter of Peter 3:15–16. Part of the trouble is the rapidity of Paul's own thought which not infrequently outruns his pen, or rather the pen of his secretary. Lines of thought can switch in mid-sentence, one idea suggests another, sentences are not always finished properly, and arguments are not always brought to a satisfactory conclusion. Some of these arguments, in any case, employ modes of reasoning which are unfamiliar to us but belong to the world of Jewish thought and tradition in which Paul had been educated at Tarsus his birthplace and at Jerusalem as a pupil of the great teacher Gamaliel.

We must also remember that, as was pointed out above, we are only reading one-half of the correspondence. Often enough, in order to know exactly what Paul is talking about, we would have to read the other half as well. It is also worth bearing in mind that Paul's letters, written as they are in response to particular needs and situations, are not fully developed statements of his teaching. We cannot get the whole picture from them. They may not always be reliable guides to where Paul himself placed the emphases in his teaching. For instance, on the strength of Romans and Galatians, many have held that the doctrine of justification by faith was paramount for St. Paul and even the central doctrine of Christianity and in the last analysis the meaning of the Gospel. The other Pauline letters and Acts suggest a broader and, so to say, a more balanced context in which to place the doctrine of justification by faith which, because of the urgent needs of a particular situation, is so stressed in Romans and Galatians. It is instructive to realize that Paul only discusses the Eucharist anywhere in his letters because he was forced to take notice of abuses regarding its celebration among the Christians of Corinth (I Cor 11:17–34).

The Letter to the Hebrews

The Letter to the Hebrews is placed at the end of the collection of St. Paul's letters but does not bear his name. It is almost certainly the work of some other unknown author. This letter seems to have been written for Christian converts from Judaism—perhaps Jewish priests—whose faith may have been wavering under the threat of persecution. It could be, too, that they were hankering after the splendors of the temple liturgy which they had lost by becoming Christians.

The writer reminds "the Hebrews" that the temple and its liturgy and its priesthood only foreshadowed Christ the High Priest and the perfect liturgy which he performs in the sanctuary of heaven. The writer exhorts them to remain steadfast in the faith following the example of holy men and women of the past.

Letters to All the Churches

There is a further collection of letters in the New Testament. These are the "Catholic Epistles" or "Letters to All the Churches." They are, for the most part, addressed to Christians generally and deal with various aspects of the Church's faith and life.

The Letter of St. James gives a number of practical instructions for Christian living. It emphasizes the need to translate one's faith into action. The First Letter of St. Peter was written to en-

courage the Christians of Asia Minor who were suffering persecution for their faith by reminding them of the great hope they
have in Christ. They are to live in a way that befits their calling.
A great part of the letter is an instruction on the sacrament of baptism. The Second Letter of St. Peter and the Letter of St. Jude
combat false teaching and the immorality resulting from it and
stress the need to hold fast to the true faith.

The First Letter of St. John is the best commentary on the
fourth Gospel. St. John also has to warn against false teachers. In
doing so he provides us with a magnificent summary of the New
Testament. God is love. His Son Jesus Christ came into this world
as a real human being to bring us into union with himself and
through him with his Father. For our part we have to love one
another. The Second and Third Letters of John are brief notes repeating one or two points of the First Letter.

Unity and Diversity

Careful reading of the New Testament letters reveals that the
early Church was far from being a uniform body. In his Letter to
the Galatians, St. Paul is having to fight against the influence of
fellow Christians who held that it is necessary to be circumcised
and observe the whole Jewish law in order to be a Christian. In
his Letter to the Colossians, there are different opponents who
were spreading angel-worship. At Corinth there were features of
local Christianity which seriously worried St. Paul and may have
tended toward what is known as "Gnosticism," whose followers
claimed to have a secret knowledge of the true meaning of Christianity. The Second Letter of John denounces as deceivers and
antichrists those who refuse to admit that Jesus Christ has come
in the flesh, and his Third Letter complains about a church leader
who refuses to accept members of John's church.

St. Paul and St. James themselves hold different theological
views, as can be seen from the use which each makes of the statement in Genesis 15:6 that Abram (Abraham) "put his faith in Yahweh, who counted this as making him justified." In Romans 4:1–
5 Paul argues from this text that Abraham was pleasing to God by
virtue of his faith alone, and not in consideration of any works.

James 2:18–24 argues from the whole relationship of Abraham with God that in his case "faith and deeds were working together; his faith became perfect by what he did," and that this is what the Genesis text really means, so that "it is by doing something good, and not only by believing, that a man is justified."

Paul and James were in communion with each other, as we know from the Letter to the Galatians 2:9, and their teachings are not in fact irreconcilable. However, there is a marked difference of emphasis, to say the least, and it even looks as if James might be deliberately arguing against Paul's interpretation of the Genesis text.

The Church, by placing both writings in the canon of the New Testament, refuses to adopt one to the exclusion of the other, but allows them to dialogue with one another. Our Catholic faith is formed by listening to both voices.

For Study or Discussion

1. How does knowing something about letter writing in the ancient world help us to understand the New Testament letters?

2. How did St Paul's "road to Damascus" experience shape the course of his life and thinking?

3. Take one of the major Pauline letters—Romans, 1 or 2 Corinthians—and pick out the topics which St. Paul discusses in it.

4. Do the New Testament letters have anything to tell us about pluralism in the Church?

18

In the End

The final book of the New Testament bridges the gap between the first generations of Christians and the second coming of Christ. This is the Book of the Apocalypse or Revelation.

The Book of Revelation rounds off the collection of sacred books which we call the Bible. It recapitulates many of the themes and images which occur in earlier books, especially the primary symbols of the Book of Genesis. It thus gives a unity and completeness to the Bible as we have it, both Old and New Testaments. At the same time, Revelation directs our attention ahead to a further completion, a final fulfillment of the self-disclosure of God, of his mighty deeds in human history, and of his companionship with human beings.

The Book of Revelation bears the name of St. John. However, it is hard to see how the same author could have produced this book and also the fourth Gospel and the First Letter of John, and scholars offer various solutions to the problem. The date at which this book was written is also not clear. Many things in the book point to the reign of the Emperor Nero (A.D. 54–68); other things suggest a date toward the end of the first century and the reign of Domitian (A.D. 81–96). Certain features of the book would favor the view that Revelation as we have it is put together out of two or more writings, perhaps by the same author, perhaps by different ones. There may well have been an earlier version of the work, written at the time of Nero, which was re-edited in the light of later events.

After an introduction consisting mainly of a letter reporting a vision of the risen Lord (chapter 1), there follow letters to each of the churches in seven cities of Asia (western Turkey). These letters are written in the name of Christ and contain messages of encouragement and warning to the leaders of the churches (chapters 2 and 3).

The rest of the book (Chapters 4–22) consists of a series of visions of the present and the future. Their style and imagery belong, as the title of the book itself suggests, to the tradition of apocalyptic writing which, we have seen, is found in some of the Old Testament prophets, as well as in books which are not included in the Bible (see Chapter Twelve of this book).

So in the Book of Revelation there is a vision of One seated on a heavenly throne surrounded by twenty-four elders and four animals (chapter 4) which recalls visions in the Books of Ezekiel (chapter 1), Daniel (7:9–10), and Isaiah (24:23). There also we find once more the Son of Man (chapter 1) already described by Daniel (7:13–14 and 10:5–6). In Revelation, too, God's holy ones are persecuted by beasts (chapter 13) which recall those seen by Daniel (chapter 7).

The Book of Revelation speaks the language of apocalyptic in order to talk about Jesus Christ and to explain his significance. He is the Son of Man of the introductory vision, who was dead and is now to live for ever and ever, and who holds the keys of death and of the underworld (1:18). The risen Jesus is the Lamb standing before the throne of God while all creatures in heaven and on earth praise him and the One seated on the throne: "You were sacrificed, and with your blood you bought men for God of every race, language, people and nation and made them a line of priests to serve our God and to rule the world" (chapter 5). So, just as the Gospels describe Jesus as the one who fulfills the law and the prophets and as Wisdom personified, Revelation describes him as the one who fulfills the visions of the apocalyptic seers.

If ever the description "cosmic drama" was deserved, it belongs to the Book of Revelation. The setting is heaven, earth, and the entire universe, and the scene changes rapidly from one to another. In heaven we assist at the ultimate liturgy, the worship of God and the Lamb by the angels and saints, a liturgy in which the Church's sacramental liturgy participates (some of the hymns sung in heaven are used in the liturgy today, and they may have originated in the liturgy of the first century).

On earth, the Church is making its way in a hostile world which attacks and persecutes it. The Book of Revelation, like earlier apocalypses such as the Book of Daniel, has a quite precise historical situation in mind, in fact the situation in which the writer is living. This is clearly a time of persecution by the authorities of the Roman empire (symbolized in the book by Babylon and by the harlot drunk on the blood of martyrs—chapter 17). The persecution is very probably that of A.D. 64 under Nero, whose name and title (Nero Caesar) when written in Hebrew characters, each of which corresponds to a number, adds up to the famous 666, the number of the beast (13:18).

As the drama unfolds, God delivers his Church from its persecutors and puts down its enemies. Babylon falls (chapter 18)—perhaps a reference to the capture of Rome by the armies of rival emperors in A.D. 69, described in terms which recall Ezekiel's description of the fall of Tyre (chapters 27–28).

The writer of Revelation sees a wider meaning in his visions than the events of his own time. This wider meaning is, however, the general situation in which the Church always finds itself, rather than particular events which still lay in the future—one should not try to find predictions of the Reformation, current world affairs, or the next great war in the pages of Revelation (or of Daniel). Nor should one try to identify the beast with any historical figure of the present or recent past.

We are to understand that in this present age the Church is continually beset by enemies. But God will always fight on its behalf. Eventually he will triumph over all the hostile powers of this world and finally over Satan, who is the first enemy and the last. The book thrills with the power of the risen Christ and with the jubilation of his Church, sure of victory over Satan and his servants Death and Hades (chapter 20).

The deliverance of the Church is the new and final exodus. Revelation makes extensive use of imagery drawn from the Book of Exodus, especially the ten plagues of Egypt (chapters 8–9; cf.

Ex 7–10), and the song of Moses after crossing the Reed Sea (chapter 15; cf. Ex 15).

But the biblical book which most clearly inspires Revelation is Genesis. The Lamb who is Jesus sacrificed and risen is the lamb that God provided for Abraham's sacrifice in place of Isaac (Gen 22). The victory over Satan is the fulfillment of God's promise to our first parents to avenge the human race on the tempter who caused their downfall (Gen 3). The woman "adorned with the sun, standing on the moon, and with the twelve stars on her head for a crown" (Rev 12) is the second Eve, while the dragon who tries to eat the child she bears is both the serpent who tempted Eve and the primeval sea monster who is the personification of chaos.

The Bible ends as it begins with creation. In Revelation, as in other apocalyptic books, the present world order is unmade. But what ensues is not the formless void but a new heaven and a new earth (chapters 21–22). God remakes the whole of creation. Paradise is regained, with the river of life and the trees of life (cf. Gen 2).

At the center of the new world is the new Jerusalem. This is the dwelling place of God among us and also the bride of the Lamb. All the hopes and longings for union with God expressed throughout the Bible are to be satisfied.

Even the New Testament is not final. Not that we await a further covenant or more biblical books. But, just as the Old Testament looked forward to its fulfillment in the New, so the New Testament looks forward to a fulfillment yet to come. Christ will return in glory, and the Church renewed and transformed will go to meet him as his Bride.

At the beginning of the Bible, God looks for Adam and Eve and calls, "Where are you?" (Gen 3:9). At the end of the Bible, the Spirit and the Bride reply, "Come" (Rev 22:17). Yes, "winter is past, the rains are over and gone" (Songs of Songs 2:11).

For Study or Discussion

1. Has the Book of Revelation anything to teach us about the present situation of the Church?

2. How does the Book of Revelation sum up the whole Bible?

3. Is there anything more to look forward to?

19

God's Book

God's Saving Word ◇ Handing On God's Word ◇ God's Written Word ◇ How God Is the Author of the Bible ◇ The Truth of Scripture

God's Saving Word

The Bible is God's book. For one thing, it is the book about God, the record of God's revelation.

God has chosen to make himself known to us. At the same time, he has shown us how we can come to him and live in union with him. God has made this saving revelation through the things he has done in human history and through the things he has said to human beings. What God has done and what he has said are equally his "word." His actions truly "speak louder than words," and his words bring about in fact what they say.

The Bible is the record of what God has said and done for our salvation. It is the book about God.

We have been looking at the various parts of this book. We have seen in the Old Testament how God, acting and speaking through the ancestors, through Moses, through the prophets and others, chose and formed a people for himself. He taught his people to acknowledge him and to wait in hope for the Savior whom he promised to send.

At last God sent his Son, his eternal Word, to live among us. Our Lord Jesus Christ has told us how God lives and how we can share his life. As the completion of his work, Christ actually rec-

147

onciled us with his Father through his passion and resurrection
and enabled us to live as God lives.

This is the New Testament, the lasting covenant between
God and the human race. God has nothing further to reveal to us
until Christ comes again in glory. On our side we owe the obedience of faith to the divine Truth who reveals himself and to the
truths which he reveals to us about himself.

Handing On God's Word

God has seen to it that his revelation would remain whole and
entire and that it would be handed on down through the ages.
After his resurrection, Christ commissioned his apostles: "Full
authority has been given to me both in heaven and on earth; go,
therefore, and make disciples of all the nations. Baptize them in
the name 'of the Father, and of the Son, and of the Holy Spirit.'
Teach them to carry out everything I have commanded you. And
know that I am with you always, until the end of the world" (Mt
28:19–20).

The apostles themselves taught what they had learned from
Jesus and also from the special instruction of the Holy Spirit (see
Jn 16:12–15). They in turn handed over to the bishops of the
Church the authority to teach in their own place. Thus through
the teaching of the bishops as the successors of the apostles, God's
saving revelation comes down to us today. This "handing on" by
the apostles and the bishops of what God has revealed for our salvation is called tradition. We shall have more to say about tradition
in the next chapter.

God's Written Word

In order to safeguard his revelation and enable it to be com-
municated to all people at all times, God has caused it to be put
into writing.

This holy writing (Scripture) is not only the record of God's
revealing and saving word. It is itself God's word, written in human words. In his written word God discloses himself to us and

brings us to salvation. By reading or listening to Scripture, we are brought into life-giving contact with God himself.

How God Is the Author of the Bible

The Bible is therefore God's word in another sense as well. God can truly be called the "author" of the whole Bible and of every part of it. That is what is meant by saying that the Bible is "inspired." St. Paul wrote: "All Scripture is inspired of God" (2 Tim 3:16) and St. Peter asserted: "Prophecy has never been put forward by man's willing it. It is rather that men impelled by the Holy Spirit have spoken under God's influence" (2 Pet 1:21).

There are many examples in the Bible itself of "divine inspiration," that is, of people who were "filled with the Holy Spirit," among them Samson (Jgs 13:25), Saul (1 Sam 10:6 and 10), the servant of Yahweh (Is 42:1), and Elizabeth (Lk 1:41). God's Spirit moved these people and others to act or speak on his behalf. Indeed he acted and spoke through them. It was in this way—by acting and speaking through men and women—that God made known his saving revelation.

In a similar way, God's Spirit moved people to write the books of Scripture. They wrote on his behalf. Really he wrote through them. It was in this way—by writing through people—that God put his saving revelation into written form.

We have seen how these books of Scripture came to be written. In some cases, many different people over a long period of time made contributions of various kinds to the book as we now have it. Some told and retold the story in spoken form, others wrote it down, still others edited the story, changed the emphasis, added details, and reflected on its meaning. God inspired all of them in their various ways to produce the books which he intended should be his written word.

The Bible is the word of God written in human words. In the composition of the books of the Bible—whether a particular book was the work of one person or of many—God chose and used human beings. They were his "instruments." But we must not think that he treated them like machines. Rather, God respected their freedom and their individuality. He made use of their own abilities and powers, which were, of course, extremely varied.

In this intimate cooperation with God, the human authors wrote all those things and only those things which God wanted written down for our salvation. Nevertheless, they were true authors, and what they wrote reflected their personal characters and their backgrounds. Thus the word of God has become fully human, just as he became a particular individual who was "like us in all things but sin."

The Truth of Scripture

The books of Scripture are the word of God, and God is Truth. It follows, as the Second Vatican Council declares, that they "teach firmly, faithfully, and without error that truth which God wanted put into the sacred writings for the sake of our salvation" (Constitution on Divine Revelation, n. 11). In saying this, the Council was echoing St. Augustine who wrote: "The Holy Spirit who spoke by the inspired writers intended to teach human beings the things profitable to salvation."

Therefore, the Bible is true. We find in it "that truth which God wanted put into the sacred writings for the sake of our salvation." Consequently, everything that is stated in the Bible for the sake of our salvation is guaranteed by God to be true. There is no possibility of error. The truthfulness of God's saving revelation is guaranteed by Truth himself, who, as St. Thomas Aquinas put it, "speaks truly, or there is nothing true."

However, the books of Scripture are also the words of human beings, and the human mind is prone to error. God kept the minds of the biblical writers free from error with regard to "that truth which he wanted put into the sacred writings for the sake of our salvation." Outside that scope, however, he makes no such guarantee of freedom from error.

It follows that in things that do not concern our salvation (such as certain historical details) there may be inaccuracies or mistakes. (However, in assessing things that look like errors in the Bible, we also need to bear in mind everything that was said in Chapter One of this book about the different kinds of writing that are to be found in the Bible.) Just as the eternal Word of God took our human nature in all its weakness, so God has adopted our human language even in its imperfections and limitations.

For Study or Discussion

1. "The Bible is the book about God." Discuss this.
2. The Bible is the book by God." Discuss this.
3. Is the Bible true?

20

The Church's Book

The Bible Entrusted to the Church

The Bible is the Church's book. God, the first Author of the Bible, has entrusted it to the Church. God has spoken his word to his Church, and the Church, like the Blessed Virgin, "stores up all these things in her heart" (Lk 2:51). The Church holds the Bible in her safekeeping, and we receive it from her hands.

What Books Belong to the Bible?

In fact, it is the Church who tells us in the first place what writings belong to the Bible. The Bible itself does not tell us. Nor do the books of the Bible bear some unmistakable stamp which enables us to recognize them at a glance as the inspired word of God. It is solely the judgment of the Church which is responsible for drawing up the list (or "Canon") of Holy Scripture.

This judgment—in which the Church was given the special assistance of the Holy Spirit—was made carefully and with much thought and discussion. It is interesting to look at the history of how the Church made up her mind about the canon of Scripture.

The Christian Church inherited the Old Testament from

the Jewish synagogue. By the time of our Lord, the Jews had gathered a large collection of writings which they recognized as divinely inspired and as a rule for their faith and life. This collection was in three main classes: the law, the prophets, and the writings.

There was, however, some discussion about which books belonged to this last, "miscellaneous" class. Around A.D. 100, the rabbis finally decided the question as far as the Jews were concerned by excluding a certain number of books which had previously been accepted by many, especially outside Palestine (Tobit, Judith, Wisdom, Ecclesiasticus, Baruch, and First and Second Maccabees, as well as parts of Esther and Daniel).

The Church had originally accepted these books, but when the Jews rejected them, many Christians felt that they should follow suit. The question was discussed for many years, the greatest saints and teachers taking opposite sides—St. Jerome was for rejecting, St. Augustine for accepting the disputed books. They were eventually accepted by the whole Church.

Of the books of the New Testament, the Gospels and St. Paul's Letters (not counting the Letter to the Hebrews) were accepted by practically everybody as Holy Scripture. There was hesitation, however, about some of the other books. In fact many "Gospels," "Acts" and "Revelations" were in circulation, some of them really heretical propaganda. By the middle of the fifth century, however, the whole Church was in agreement in accepting the twenty-seven books of the New Testament as we have them.

For over one thousand years the Church was practically free from argument about the canon of Scripture. Controversy was revived in the sixteenth century, when the Protestant reformers decided to go back to the Jewish canon for the Old Testament. (That is why, if you pick up a "Protestant Bible," you will find some of the Old Testament books missing, or else printed separately under the heading "Apocrypha.")

The Council of Trent solemnly declared that all the books in the traditional list of both the Old and the New Testaments, together with all their parts, are sacred and canonical.

The Bible in the Church

There are other ways too in which the Bible is the Church's Book. The Church herself lives by the word of God. You could even say that she lives on it. God's word is her food.

Therefore, the Church is nourished in her faith and life by the Bible which is the written word of God. That is why, for instance, the reading of the Scriptures forms an integral part of every act of the Church's liturgy. The Church constantly sustains and renews her faith and teaching with Holy Scripture. She listens to what God has to say to her in the Scriptures, so as to carry it out, like the Virgin Mary, who heard the word of God and acted upon it (see Lk 8:21).

Understanding the Bible

The Church, therefore, is not above the Bible. She is, however, the proper interpreter of the Bible. She knows what it means. Another way of putting this is that the Bible must be read in the Church and with the Church. It must be read in communion with her faith and life and worship and, in the last analysis, in submission to her authoritative judgment.

Individual Christians reading the Bible have the help of the Holy Spirit assisting them to understand God's written word. Therefore they can read the Scriptures with confidence and assurance. All the same, they do not simply rely on their own judgment as to the meaning of what they read. The Holy Spirit, who is the Spirit of unity, leads them to seek the communion of belief which is to be found in the Church.

Scholars, too, have not finished their work when they have amassed all the information which literary and historical studies can supply. These sciences, as we have seen, throw much valuable light on the Bible, and we cannot do without them. However, literary and historical research is not enough in itself to understand the Bible.

In order to understand the Bible properly, we must also read it in the light of the Church's tradition. This means, on the one hand, paying attention to the way it has been understood in the past by the great teachers and interpreters of the Bible in every period of the Church's history, especially by the Fathers of the early Church, who were closer to the world of the Bible and to the mentality of its authors. It also means looking to the whole of the Church's faith and life and worship down through the ages to the present day. This will very often reveal clearly how the Church has understood a particular passage which is otherwise obscure or doubtful.

In fact, we Catholics do not derive our faith from the Bible, but rather we find our faith in the Bible. The word of God is conveyed by the Scriptures, but not exclusively by them. It is conveyed also by the memory of the Church constantly recalled in teaching, in liturgy and in practical action. And it is conveyed even today by those who speak with a prophetic voice or who can discern the "signs of the times." Our faith is formed by all of these and is found in all of them—not just one independently of the others, but all of them as they function within the unity of the Church and as they test and verify one another. Among them the Scriptures do have a special place as the written word of God, and therefore a permanently available witness against which the others can be tested. On the other hand, a book is "alive" only when it is being interpreted and understood, that is, in the case of the Bible, by the living tradition of the Church.

We are, therefore, in living continuity with earlier generations of Catholic Christians. This does not mean that we must always understand a particular passage of Scripture in the same way as they did. We do not derive our faith from past interpretations of the Bible. On the other hand, the faith that we find in the Scriptures today we find also in the faith found there by the Church in past ages. The same word is spoken to us as to them, and the same Spirit who inspired the speaking and the writing down of that Word has been guiding people in every age "into all truth," that is, into an authentic understanding of the Scriptures (see Jn 16:13).

If necessary, the teaching authority of the Church may declare what is the true meaning of a passage of Scripture. Such declarations, by a Pope or an ecumenical council, are rare. However, various Popes, as well as the Second Vatican Council, have issued authoritative guidance on how to go about understanding the Bible. There is also a Pontifical Biblical Commission which is entrusted by the Pope with supervising the study and interpretation of the Bible.

God's Living Word

In Holy Scripture God has spoken and still speaks to us—to individuals as well as to his people as a whole.

The word of God is not like any other word. It is "living and effective, sharper than any two-edged sword. It penetrates and divides soul and spirit, joints and marrow; it judges the reflections and thoughts of the heart" (Heb 4:12). Thus, to hear God's word is to allow oneself to be judged by it.

God's word actually brings about what it says. As God himself declares through the prophet Isaiah: "So shall my word be that goes forth from my mouth; it shall not return to me void, but shall do my will, achieving the end for which I sent it" (55:11). In the beginning God made heaven and earth by his word (see Gen 1 and Jn 1). His word is still creating. His command still "calls into being those things which had not been" (Rom 4:17). Therefore to hear God's word is to allow oneself to be changed by it.

We hear God's word whenever we listen to the Scriptures proclaimed in the liturgy. We "hear" it also whenever we read the Bible ourselves. As we listen to the Scriptures or read them, Christ, who is himself the Word of God, becomes present to us. To get to know the Scriptures is to get to know Christ.

For Study or Discussion

1. Is the Church above the Bible?
2. How do we know which books belong to the Bible?
3. How does the Holy Spirit help us to understand the Bible?
4. What can we learn from the Blessed Virgin about reading or listening to the Bible?

For Further Reading

A. The Whole Bible

The Jerusalem Bible, Standard Edition, London: Darton, Longman and Todd, 1966. The introductions to the various sections of the Bible and to many of the individual books, as well as the footnotes and references, make this edition a Bible and Commentary in one volume. New and revised edition 1985.

Harrington, Wilfrid J., O.P., *Key to the Bible*, Garden City, New York: Image Books, Doubleday and Co., 1976 (also London and Dublin: Geoffrey Chapman, 1965) in three volumes: Vol. 1, *Record of Revelation;* Vol. 2, *The Old Testament: Record of the Promise;* Vol. 3, *The New Testament: Record of Fulfillment.*

Jerome Biblical Commentary, Englewood Cliffs, N.J.: Prentice-Hall, 1968 (eds. R.E. Brown, Joseph A. Fitzmyer, and R.E. Murphy). New and revised edition in preparation.

New Catholic Commentary on Holy Scripture, London: Nelson, 1969 (eds. Reginald C. Fuller, L. Johnston, and C. Kearns).

McKenzie, John L., S.J., *Dictionary of the Bible*, Milwaukee: Bruce, 1965.

The Bible Today, periodical published by The Liturgical Press, Collegeville, Minn., which enables the non-expert to keep up with biblical scholarship in many fields.

B. Chapter 1

Aharoni, Yohanan, *The Archaeology of the Land of Israel*, Philadelphia: Westminister Press, 1982.

Aharoni, Y. and Avi-Yonah, M., *The Macmillan Bible Atlas*, New York: Macmillan, 1968.

Guides to Biblical Scholarship, paperback series: New Testament Guides, ed. by Dan O. Via, Jr., Old Testament Guides, ed. by J. Coert Rylaarsdam, Philadelphia: Fortress Press, 1970-. These short books deal with topics like textual and literary criticism. Some will be referred to below.

Pritchard, James, *The Ancient Near East: An Anthology of Texts and Pictures*, Princeton, N.J.: Princeton Univ. Press, 1965.

C. Old Testament in General

Anderson, B.W., *Understanding the Old Testament*, 3rd revised edition, Englewood Cliffs, N.J.: Prentice-Hall, 1979.

Boadt, Lawrence, C.S.P., *Reading the Old Testament: An Introduction*, New York, N.Y./Mahwah, N.J.: Paulist Press, 1984.

Collegeville Old Testament Commentary, Collegeville, Minn.: Liturgical Press, 1984-. This is a new series which has begun to appear.

Ellis, Peter F., C.SS.R., *The Men and the Message of the Old Testament*, 3rd edition, Collegeville, Minn.: Liturgical Press, 1975.

Jensen, Joseph, O.S.B., *God's Word to Israel*, revised edition, Wilmington, Del.: Michael Glazier, 1982.

Old Testament Message: A Biblical-Theological Commentary, Wilmington, Del.: Michael Glazier, 1982–84 (series).

D. Chapters 2 to 4

Bailey, Lloyd, *The Pentateuch*, Nashville: Abingdon Press, 1981.

L'Heureux, Conrad, *In and Out of Paradise*, Ramsey, N.J.: Paulist Press, 1983.

McCarthy, Dennis, S.J., *Old Testament Covenant: A Survey of Current Opinions*, Atlanta: John Knox Press, 1972.

Newman, Murray, *The People of the Covenant*, Nashville: Abingdon Press, 1962.

Vawter, Bruce, *On Genesis: A New Reading*, New York: Doubleday, 1977

E. Chapters 5 and 6

Bright, John, *A History of Israel*, 3rd edition, Philadelphia: Westminster Press, 1981.

De Vaux, Roland, *Ancient Israel, Its Life and Institutions* (Eng. tr. John McHugh), New York: McGraw-Hill, 1961.

Hayes, J. and Miller, J. Maxwell (eds.), *Israelite and Judean History*, Philadelphia: Westminster Press, 1977.

Kraus, Hans-Joachim, *Worship in Israel*, Atlanta: John Knox Press, 1966.

F. Chapters 7 to 9

Ackroyd, Peter, *Exile and Restoration: A Study of Hebrew Thought of the Sixth Century B.C.*, Philadelphia: Westminster Press, 1968.

Bickerman, E., *From Ezra to the Last of the Maccabees: Foundations of Postbiblical Judaism*, New York: Schocken Books, 1947.

Foerster, W., *From the Exile to Christ*, Philadelphia: Fortress Press, 1964.

Raitt, Thomas M., *A Theology of Exile: Judgment-Deliverance in Jeremiah and Ezekiel*, Philadelphia: Fortress Press, 1977.

G. Chapter 10

Anderson, B.W., *Out of the Depths: The Psalms Speak for Us Today*, revised edition, Philadelphia: Westminster Press, 1982.

Guthrie, Harvey, *Israel's Sacred Songs,* New York: Seabury Press, 1966.

Lewis, C.S., *Reflections on the Psalms,* London: Geoffrey Bles, 1958.

Ringren, Helmer, *The Faith of the Psalmists,* London: SCM Press, 1963.

Sabourin, Leopold, *The Psalms, Their Origin and Meaning* (two vols.), New York: Alba House, 1969.

H. Chapter 11

Boadt, Lawrence, C.S.P., *Wisdom Literature and Proverbs,* Collegeville, Minn.: Liturgical Press, 1984.

Crenshaw, James, *Old Testament Wisdom: An Introduction,* Atlanta, John Knox Press, 1981.

Scott, R.B.Y., *The Way of Wisdom in the Old Testament,* New York: Macmillan, 1971.

Von Rad, Gerhard, *Wisdom in Israel,* Nashville: Abingdon Press, 1972.

I. Chapter 12

Morris, Leon, *Apocalyptic,* Grand Rapids, Michigan: Eerdmans, 1972.

Reid, David P., *What Are They Saying About the Prophets?* New York: Paulist Press, 1980.

Russell, D.S., *Apocalyptic Ancient and Modern,* Philadelphia: Fortress Press, 1978.

Scott, R.B.Y., *The Relevance of the Prophets,* New York: Macmillan, 1967.

Von Rad, Gerhard, *The Message of the Prophets,* New York: Harper and Row, 1968.

Winward, Stephen, *A Guide to the Prophets,* Atlanta: John Knox Press, 1976.

J. New Testament in General and Chapters 13 and 14

Barrett, C.K., *The New Testament Background: Selected Documents,* New York: Harper and Row, 1961.

Grant, M., *The World of Rome,* Cleveland: World, 1960.

Jones, A.H.M., *The Herods of Judaea,* Oxford: Clarendon Press, 1938.

McKenzie, John L., S.J., *The Power and the Wisdom: An Interpretation of the New Testament,* Milwaukee: Bruce, 1965.

New Testament Message: A Biblical-Theological Commentary, Wilmington, Del.: Michael Glazier, 1979–1980 (series).

Russell, D.S., *Between the Testaments,* Philadelphia: Fortress Press, 1979.

Sabourin, Leopold, *The Bible and Christ: The Unity of the Two Testaments,* New York: Alba House, 1980.

K. Chapter 15

(a) General

Dodd, C.H., *The Apostolic Preaching and Its Development,* London: Hodder and Stoughton, 1949.

Dodd, C.H., *The Parables of the Kingdom,* London: Nisbet, 1943.

Hendrickx, H., *The Infancy Narratives,* Manila, Philippines: East Asian Pastoral Institute, 1975.

Hendrickx, H., *The Passion Narratives of the Synoptic Gospels,* Manila, Philippines: East Asian Pastoral Institute, 1975.

Hendrickx, H., *The Resurrection Narratives of the Synoptic Gospels,* Manila, Philippines: East Asian Pastoral Institute, 1978.

Hendrickx, H., *Sermon on the Mount,* Manila, Philippines: East Asian Pastoral Institute, 1979.

Léon-Dufour, Xavier, *The Gospels and the Jesus of History* (Eng. tr. John McHugh), London: Collins (Fontana), 1968.

Moule, C.F.D., *The Birth of the New Testament*, London: A. and C. Black, 1962.

(b) Matthew

Beare, F.W., *The Gospel According to Matthew*, Oxford: Blackwell, 1981.

Meier, John P., *The Vision of Matthew: Christ, Church and Morality in the First Gospel*, New York/Ramsey/Toronto: Paulist Press, 1979.

Viviano, B.T., *The Kingdom of God in History*, Wilmington, Del.: Glazier, 1986.

(c) Mark

Keegan, Terence J., *A Commentary on the Gospel of Mark*, New York/Ramsey/Toronto: Paulist Press, 1981.

Martin, R.P., *Mark, Evangelist and Theologian*, Exeter: Paternoster, 1972.

Rhoads, David and Michie, Donald, *Mark as Story: An Introduction to the Narrative of a Gospel*, Philadelphia: Fortress Press, 1982.

(d) Luke

Cassidy, R.J., *Jesus, Politics and Society: A Study of Luke's Gospel*, Maryknoll, N.Y.: Orbis, 1978.

Kealy, John P., *Luke's Gospel Today*, Denville, N.J.: Dimension Books, 1979.

Marshall, I. Howard, *Luke, Historian and Theologian*, Exeter: Paternoster, 1970.

(e) John

Brown, Raymond E., *The Gospel According to John* (2 vols.), Garden City, N.Y.: Doubleday, 1966 and 1970.

Hunter, A.M., *According to John*, London: SCM Press, 1968.

Smalley, S., John, *Evangelist and Interpreter*, Exeter: Paternoster, 1978.

L. Chapter 16

Dupont, J., *The Salvation of the Gentiles, Studies in the Acts of the Apostles* (Eng. tr. J.R. Keating), New York/Ramsey/Toronto: Paulist Press, 1979.

Karris, Robert J., *What Are They Saying About Luke and Acts?* New York: Paulist Press, 1979.

M. Chapter 17

Amiot, F., *The Key Concepts of St Paul* (Eng. tr. J. Dingle), New York: Herder and Herder, 1962.

Dodd, C.H., *The Meaning of Paul for Today*, New York: Meridian, 1957.

Doty, W., *Letters in Primitive Christianity*, Philadelphia: Fortress Press, 1973.

Murphy-O'Connor, J., *Becoming Human Together: The Pastoral Anthropology of St Paul*, 2nd revised edition, Wilmington, Del.: Glazier, 1982.

N. Chapter 18

Harrington, Wilfrid J., *The Apocalypse of St. John, A Commentary*, London: Chapman, 1969.

Pilch, J., *What Are They Saying About the Book of Revelation?* New York: Paulist Press, 1978.

O. Chapters 19 and 20

Benoit, Pierre, *Inspiration and the Bible* (Eng. tr. J. Murphy-O'Connor and Sister M. Keverne), London/New York: Sheed and Ward, 1965.

Keegan, Terence J., *Interpreting the Bible: A Popular Introduction to Hermeneutics*, New York/Mahwah: Paulist Press, 1985.

Vatican Council II, Dogmatic Constitution *Dei Verbum* on Divine
    Revelation (no. 58 in *Vatican Council II: Conciliar and Post-
    Conciliar Documents*, ed. Austin Flannery, Collegeville, Minn.:
    Liturgical Press, 1975).